Goode's World Atlas, © Copyright 1990 by Rand McNally & Company, R.L. 90-S-57

Scale 1:40 000 000; one inch to 630 miles. Lambert's Azimuthal, Equal Area Projection

Elevations and depressions are given in feet.

New International Atlas, © Copyright 1990 by
Rand McNally & Company, R.L. 90-S-57

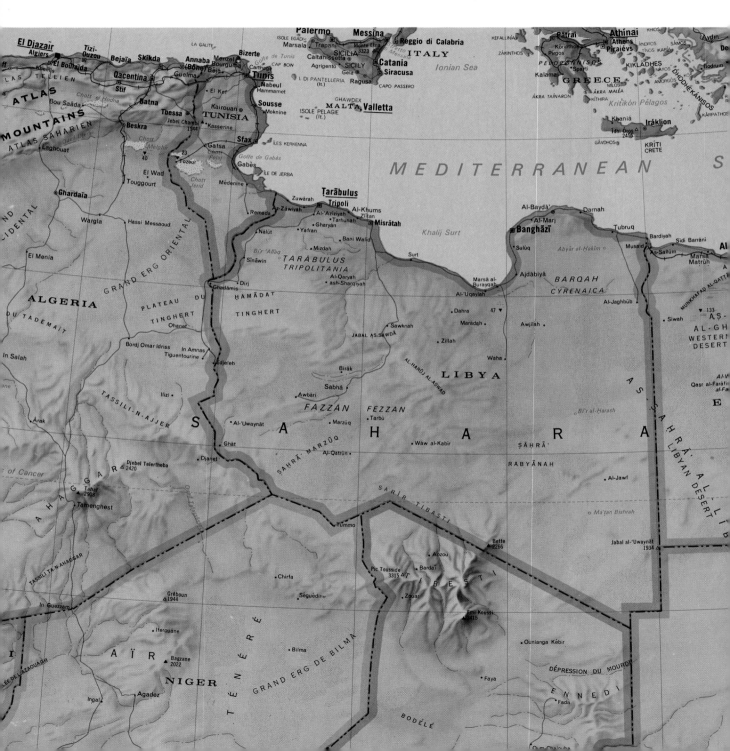

El Djazaïr
Algiers
El Boulaïda
Tizi-Ouzou
Bejaïa
Skikda
Annaba
(Bône)
Menzel
Bourguiba
Bizerte
Guelma
Qacentina
Stif
Batna
Tbessa
El Ket
Béja
Tunis
Nabeul
Hammamet

ATLAS
MOUNTAINS
Bou Saâda
Chott el Hodna
Kairouan
Sousse
Moknine
TUNISIA

ATLAS SAHARIEN
Beskra
Jebel Chambi
1544
Kasserine
Laghouat
Chott
Melghir
Gafsa
Chott
Fejaj
Sfax
ÎLES KERKENNA

23
40
Tozeur

Ghardaïa
El Wad
Touggourt
Chott Jerid
Gabès
Médenine
ÎLE DE JERBA
Golfe de Gabès

Wargla
Hassi Messaoud
Zuwärah
Zlītan
Al-Khums
Ţarābulus
Tripoli

El Menia
Remada
Az-Zāwiyah
Al-'Azīzīyah
Tarhūnah
Gharyān
Misrātah
Khalīj Surt
Al-Baydā'
Al-Marj
Darnah
Tubruq
Bardiyah
Sidi Barrāni

Nälüt
Yafran
Bani Walid
Banghāzī
Sulūq
Musaid
Al-Sallūm
Marsā
Matrūh

Bīr 'Allāq
Mizdah
Surt
Ajdābiyā
Suluq
Abyār al-Hakīm
BARQAH
CYRENAICA
Al-Jaghbūb

Sīnāwin
TARĀBULUS
TRIPOLITANIA
Marsā al-
Burayqah
Al-'Uqaylah

ALGERIA
Ghadāmis
Dirj
Dahra
47
Marādah
Awjilah
Siwah
AS-
AL-GH
WESTERN
DESERT

DU TADEMAÏT
Ohanet
HAMĀDAT
TINGHERT
TINGHERT

In Salah
Bordj Omar Idriss
In Amnas
Tiguentourine
Sawknah
JABAL AS-SAWDĀ
Zillah
Waha
Qasr al-Farāfi
al-Fa

TASSILI-N-AJJER
Edjeleh
Birāk
Al-HARŪJ AL-ASWAD
LIBYA

Ilizi
Sabhā
Bīr al-Harash

Àrak
Awbāri
FAZZĀN
FEZZAN
Tarbū

of Cancer
Al-'Uwaynāt
Marzūq
Wāw al-Kabir
SĀHRĀ
RABYĀNAH
Al-Jawf

Djebel Telertheba
2420
Ghāt
Al-Qatrūn

Tahat
2908
Tamenghest
Djanet

TASSILI TA-N-AHAGGAR
SARĪR TIBASTI
o Ma'tan Bishrah

In Guezzam
Tümmo
Bette
2266
Jabal al-'Uwaynāt
1934

Chirfa
Aozou
Bardaï
Pic Tousside
3315

Gréboun
1944
Séguédine
Zouar

Iferouane
Bilma
Emi Koussi
3415
TIBESTI

AÏR
Bagzane
2022
Ounianga Kébir
DÉPRESSION DU MOURDI

NIGER
GRAND ERG DE BILMA
Faya
ENNEDI
Fada

Ingal
Agadez
BODÉLÉ

MEDITERRANEAN S

Palermo
Messina
Reggio di Calabria
ITALY
Ionian Sea
KEFALLINÍA
Pátrai
Athínai
Athens
Piraiévs

Marsala
Trapani
Monte Etna
3323
Catania
Siracusa
Zákinthos
Kórinthos
Sparti
ÁNDROS
SÁMOS
Aydin
De

Caltanissetta
SICILY
Gela
Ragusa
CAPO PASSERO
ÁKRA TAÍNARON
ÁKRA MALÉA
Kíthira
KÍKLADHES
NÁXOS
DHODHEKÁNISOS
AMORGÓS
Bodrum

I. DI PANTELLERIA
(It.)
GREECE
Kritikón Pélagos
KÁRPATHOS

GHAWDEX
MALTA
Valletta
ISOLE PELAGIE
(It.)
Khaniá
Irāklion
Ídhi Óros
2456
KRÍTI
CRETE
GÁVDHOS

CAP BON
Golfe de Tunis
ISOLE EGADI

# Enchantment of the World
# TUNISIA

*By Mary Virginia Fox*

**Consultant for Tunisia:** Robert Mortimer, Ph.D., Department of Political
Science, Haverford College, Haverford, Pennsylvania

**Consultant for Reading:** Robert L. Hillerich, Ph.D., Bowling Green State
University, Bowling Green, Ohio

**CHILDRENS PRESS®**
CHICAGO

*Nomads and visitors at an oasis in the desert*

Library of Congress Cataloging-in-Publication Data

Fox, Mary Virginia.
    Tunisia / by Mary Virginia Fox.
        p.    cm. — (Enchantment of the world)
    Summary: Discusses the geography, history, people, and
culture of Tunisia, a land of contrasts.
    Includes index.
    ISBN 0-516-02724-7
    1.  Tunisia—Juvenile literature.  [1.  Tunisia.]
I. Title. II. Series.
DT245.F69   1990                                    90-2199
961.1—dc20                                              CIP
                                                        AC

**Picture Acknowledgments**
**The Bettmann Archive:** 15 (right), 16 (2 photos), 17
(2 photos), 27, 34, 36
© **Cameramann International, Ltd.:** 9 (top left and right),
41, 54 (2 photos), 55 (right), 56 (left), 58 (left), 59 (right),
63 (right), 83 (right), 86 (right), 93, 100 (left and top right),
102 (right), 104, 106, 107 (right)
© **John Elk III:** 31, 61 (top), 66, 68 (top right), 76
© **Virginia Grimes:** 24
**Historical Picture Service, Chicago:** 39 (2 photos)
**Journalism Services:** © **Gill S. J. Copeland,** 11, 72, 74
(bottom)
© **Jason Lauré:** 4, 10 (right), 61 (bottom), 62 (2 photos),
63 (left), 65, 67 (right), 79, 96, 103
**North Wind Picture Archives:** 15 (left), 26
**Photri:** 9 (bottom left), 10 (left), 68 (bottom), 88
**H. Armstrong Roberts:** 94 (left); © **M. Thonig,** Cover, 30,
94 (right); © **Geopress,** 18; © **Helbig/Zefa,** 64 (right)
**Root Resources:** © **Jane P. Downton,** 56 (right), 73
(bottom), 74 (top left); © **Irene E. Hubbell,** 59 (left), 90
(bottom right), 100 (center and bottom right); © **Vera
Bradshaw,** 107 (left)
**Shostal Associates/SuperStock International, Inc.:** 6, 12,
52, 55 (left), 57, 58 (right), 64 (left), 77, 90 (left), 116;
© **G. Ricatto,** 5; © **Hubertus Kanus,** 8, 82 (left), 98 (left),
118; © **A. Tessore,** 67 (left); © **George Hunter,** 70;
© **David Warren,** 82 (right), 97; © **William L. Hamilton,**
91 (left)
**Third Coast Stock Source:** © **Ted H. Funk,** 20
(right), 68 (top left), 74 (top right), 86 (left), 90 (top right),
91 (right), 98 (right), 102 (left)
**UPI/Bettmann Newsphotos:** 33, 44 (2 photos), 45
(2 photos), 46, 49, 51
**Valan:** © **Val & Alan Wilkinson,** 20 (left), 73 (top), 81, 83
(left), 98 (center); © **Aubrey Diem,** 84
**Len W. Meents:** Maps on 53, 61, 63, 65, 69, 71, 77
**Courtesy Flag Research Center, Winchester,
Massachusetts 01890:** Flag on back cover
**Cover:** Small street near Tunis, Tunisia

*A lemonade stand in Sidi Bou Said*

## TABLE OF CONTENTS

*Tunisians wear traditional and contemporary clothing. The woman on the right most likely is wearing Western clothes under her* sifsari.

# Chapter 1
# LAND OF CONTRASTS

Tunisia is a mosaic of a dozen races and cultures—and each retains its individuality. There are those who work with computers to update the landing procedures at modern airports and there are Tunisians who live in tents and migrate with herds of sheep and camels far from city streets. There are women who wear the latest Paris fashions and women who tattoo their faces and wear veils to hide from strangers.

It is a country rich in tradition, but a country where traditions have changed with each wave of invaders who have left skills and religions behind. Tunisia is Arab by culture, African by geography, and politically its people support a Socialist government. It is a land of surprises and contrasts.

## MOUNTAINS, DESERT, AND SEA

Tunisia is a wedge of land between the larger Arab countries of Algeria to the west and Libya to the east. This part of the North African coast is called the Maghrib, which literally means "the

*A few olive trees and meager pastureland in the Tunisian Dorsale chain*

west.'' The Maghrib is commonly thought of as ''an island'' or land between the ''sea of sand,'' the Sahara desert, and the Mediterranean Sea.

The Tunisian coast juts out into the Mediterranean, pinching the sea into an 85-mile (137-kilometer) passage between Tunisia and the island of Sicily. The country is located halfway between Gibraltar and Suez, which made it an important link in the trade routes of the world even before history was written.

Most of northern Tunisia is mountainous. It is no match for the scale of the Atlas Mountains in Algeria, but the highest peak of the Tunisian Dorsale chain still reaches an impressive 5,000 feet (1,524 meters). The mountain ridges slant northeastward across the country, ending in the sea at Cap Bon. These mountains lift the prevailing northwesterly winds and squeeze the moisture from the air, giving the corner of Tunisia next to Algeria and the coast an ample supply of water.

This region is called the *Tell*. It is deeply cut by the Majardah

*Above: An irrigation pump on the Majardah River, the only Tunisian river with water year round. Left, top and bottom: Tunis, the capital, is a combination of new and old.*

River, which is the only river in all of Tunisia to have water year round. The mountains are covered by forests of juniper, laurel, and myrtle, as well as a type of oak whose bark is harvested for cork products. Wild boar roam the forests and are hunted for sport as well as food.

The Tell has the richest soil and the heaviest population. It is here along the coast that succeeding generations of settlers have built their cities, sometimes one on top of another, as each one was destroyed by invaders. Most of the cities along the coast now bear a strong resemblance to their European counterparts across the Mediterranean.

The capital, Tunis, is a combination of the old and new. Winter brings damp, uncomfortable weather. Only recently have modern buildings been equipped with central heating to ease the discomfort, but during the rest of the year the weather is pleasant. Tourism has developed into a profitable industry.

From the Gulf of Tunis, past Cap Bon, the coastline heads south

*Left: Boats off Tunisia's Mediterranean coast*
*Right: A couple watches the surf roll in near the port of Carthage*

in an S curve, with two other bays that have been busy harbors since the beginning of travel on water. This area is known as the *Sahil,* which is the Arabic word for coast.

Everywhere there are sandy beaches, but none exactly the same. At Cap Bon they are bordered by orange and lemon groves and stands of jasmine. Their blossoms are distilled to extract oils from which perfumes are made.

At Sousse and at Monastir, olive trees and the first palm groves are found. All along these shores there are islands, some rocky and wild, like La Galite and Zembra. Others, such as Kerkenna and Djerba, are quite flat with palm trees and hotels for the thousands of tourists who come each year.

There is a theory that the islands of Djerba and Kerkenna are all that is left of the lost continent of Atlantis, which some people believe was submerged by a gigantic tidal wave during ancient times. It is true they are barely above the waters of the sea, but geologists have yet to prove this early history.

There is little rain here, but the climate of the Sahil is affected by the humidity of the sea. Heavy dews make it possible to raise large olive groves. Some of the trees are hundreds of years old, it is said, and still producing.

*In the south, Berber dwellings are carved out of the rocks.*

The coast provides another harvest. Fishing is an important part of the life of the Sahil, fish for food and sponges for export.

The central part of Tunisia is called the *Steppe*, high or low steppe according to elevation—the highest being near the Algerian border. The soil is poor, the rainfall scanty and unpredictable. Very few crops can be raised in this area. The only cash crop is esparto grass, which grows wild. It is harvested for paper and the manufacture of rope. The land is used for pasture, but sheep, goats, and camels find meager rations here.

In the extreme south the land rises to form plateaus and eroded hills. In the winter occasional downpours gash the land in deep furrows, but in summer fields bake. This is where the land shifts into the waste of the Sahara desert. "The country of hardships," it is called.

There are occasional salt flats, or *chotts*, that fill with water in the winter, but the runoff only sours the soil and kills any

11

*Soil erosion in the desert*

greening plants. Most of the year the chotts are only dead salt-crusted plains, the bleakest desert.

The interior of southern Tunisia is almost totally empty of people, animals, and vegetation. Temperature changes are enormous. In daylight hours the sun bakes the rocky land, creating shimmering mirages that mock the desolation with visions of water. At dusk temperatures drop, making it possible for the hardy to travel between the few oases. Even in the coldest months, the freezing point is rarely reached except at high elevations, but dreaded windstorms bring about blinding blizzards of sand.

The oases are the difference between life and death for the south.

Saharan species, such as acacia and saltbush, grow wild. At higher levels occasional patches of scrub grass provide meager food for camels.

The climate and geography of the land dictate what life is like in Tunisia. That is why there are such extreme differences.

# Chapter 2

# QUEEN DIDO AND

# THE OX HIDE

The Phoenicians were the first to develop the potential of Tunisia and the bordering sea, but they did not move into an empty land. This part of North Africa was occupied by people first known as Numidians and later called Berbers from the Greek word *barberio*, meaning barbarians. Their origin is a mystery. They were of the Caucasian race, usually stocky in appearance and, surprisingly, often light in coloring, with blue eyes.

It is hard to sort fact from legend in the early history of Tunisia. Phoenicians had already set up city-states along the eastern shores of the Mediterranean. It is said that Queen Elissa fled from Tyre, in the country we now call Lebanon, to escape her murderous brother King Pygmalion. She was accompanied by priests and servants in search of a new place to settle.

When she came to a fine harbor surrounded by highlands, she is said to have bargained with the Berbers for as much land as could be covered by an ox hide. By cutting the hide in narrow strips and tying them together, she had a rope long enough to encircle the hill of Carthage. The bargain was kept, the land was hers. She became known to Western readers through Virgil's *Aeneid* as Queen Dido.

As nearly as archaeologists and historians can guess, the date was about 814 B.C. What we now know as Tunisia, with its strategic location and great harbors, soon became the stronghold of the Phoenicians for several centuries to come. It was then called *Ifriqiya*.

## EXPLORERS AND TRADERS

The Phoenicians were shipbuilders, explorers, and traders. Their broad-beamed, chunky ships with horse-head prows sailed waters far from home. They ventured out into the dangerous unknown waters of the Atlantic, as far north as the British Isles and as far south as to circle the continent of Africa.

World trade even then was based on the value of precious metals. Silver was found in Spain, gold in Africa, tin came from Britain, and lead and iron from Europe. Yet it also has been recorded that ivory, cyprus wood, precious stones, oil, honey, wine, fine linen, and wool were often part of the Phoenicians' cargoes. Their special purple dye made from an extract of seashells was so highly prized it is still known as the royal color.

As world travelers, the Phoenicians spread their skill and knowledge. They taught the Hebrews how to build temples, the Romans how to fight at sea, and the Greeks how to write with phonetic characters. This is one of the greatest accomplishments we are still enjoying today.

There were twenty-two Phoenician symbols, each standing for a distinctive sound, in contrast to the picture signs, the hieroglyphs, of the Egyptians. Their alphabet was easily transferable from one language to another. Even our computer language of today is derived from the Phoenician script.

| English | Phœnician |
|---------|-----------|
| A | 𐤀 |
| B | 𐤁 |
| C G | 𐤂 |
| D | △ |
| E | 𐤄 |
| F V | 𐤅 |
| G Z | 𐤆 |
| H | 𐤇 𐤈 |
| I | 𐤉 |
| K | 𐤊 |
| L | 𐤋 |
| M | 𐤌 |
| N | 𐤍 𐤎 |
| O | O |
| P | 𐤐 𐤑 |
| Q | 𐤒 |
| R | 𐤓 |
| S | 𐤔 |
| T | X |

*Right: The English and Phoenician alphabets*
*Above: The Phoenicians landing on Cyprus, one of their colonies*

Phoenicians were the first to mass-produce transparent glass. Three thousand years ago they were able to make sweet water from the seabed in a filtration process that still commands the respect of modern engineers.

They were fierce fighters when need be, but the Phoenicians gained their power by tying together widely scattered colonies and controlling their trade. They collected taxes and recruited the Berbers for their paid armies, which were mustered to keep jealous neighbors from taking over the trading routes they had established. They rarely pursued war to gain land, only to gain power.

It was their mighty display of sea power that kept their rivals at a distance. In addition to their deep-bellied cargo ships, they maintained a fighting fleet. The largest of these had five banks of oars on each side. Prows were fitted with sharp beaks or battering rams. Their captains were the most skilled in the world.

*Right: A bust of Hannibal*
*Above: Hannibal's army, which included*
*many Berbers, attacked the Romans.*

Rome had a superb army, but had no navy to match the Carthaginians'. The Romans set out to capture one of the Phoenicians' huge fighting ships to use as a model for their own fleet. Luck was with them. Overpowered in a storm, the Romans had their prize, a *quiquereme*, a five-deck ship. In two months, it is said, they had copied it plank for plank and had built a hundred more like it. The year was 265 B.C. Now was the time for Phoenician power to be tested.

## WAR WITH ROME

The growth of Phoenician trade in Italy and in the western Mediterranean brought about a confrontation with the growing power of Rome in the third century B.C. Carthage was defeated in the first of the Punic Wars in 264-241 B.C. and was forced to give up its colonies in Sicily and Sardinia (present-day Italian islands). This did not stop Carthage from expanding in another direction. The Phoenicians rapidly built a new and larger empire in Spain.

*Roman troops attacked (left), seized (right), and destroyed Carthage.*

To keep the Romans from constantly interfering in their colonial affairs, Carthaginian General Hannibal led an army of fifty-nine thousand, many of them Berbers, out of Spain and across the Alps into Italy with a baggage train of elephants. Hannibal defeated the Roman army in three battles, but was never able to capture Rome.

In retaliation, Roman troops moved against Carthaginian strongholds in Spain and northern Africa, finally defeating them in 202 B.C. The Phoenician fleet was burned and Phoenician territory was occupied, except for a small section of north and eastern Tunisia.

Carthage tried one more time in 149 B.C. to fight the Romans in Numidia (now Algeria). Its army was slaughtered. Carthage was destroyed, buildings burned, and salt plowed into fertile soil by the Romans.

*Ruins of the Roman forum at Thuborbo Majus, about
fifty miles (eighty kilometers) southwest of Tunis*

# Chapter 3

# ROMAN RULE

---

The Carthaginian territory was now annexed to Rome and organized as a Roman province governed by a civilian official appointed by the Roman Senate. The land was far too valuable to be kept idle. Julius Caesar finally ordered the rebuilding of Carthage and other cities on the coast of Tunisia.

It was done in an orderly fashion. Streets were laid out in characteristic grid design. Forums to hold public meetings, marketplaces, and public baths were built. Fountains graced the cities. Beautiful mosaics decorated private as well as public buildings. Some of the mosaics now displayed in the Bardo Museum in Tunis give us a graphic, sometimes humorous, picture of life during Roman times. One depicts a mother scolding a tardy child; another, a slave asleep under a palm tree; and several show victorious battles fought with swords and daggers.

The Roman love of cruel gladiator games and human and animal torture were carried out in colosseums that rivaled the size of any but the one in Rome. It was a part of ancient culture we abhor today, but natural for the Phoenician/Berber society to accept. The Phoenicians themselves were known to have used human sacrifice, particularly first-born children, as part of their religious rites. It was not until Christianity began seeping across borders that an end was put to the bloody games.

*Roman aqueducts (left) are still used for irrigation.*
*A paved Roman road in the ruins at Carthage (right)*

Paved roads with mileposts every thousand paces (*mille passius*), or 4,584 feet (1,397 meters), linked all parts of the African Roman empire. During recent floods, Roman-built bridges survived in Tunisia. Bridges built by modern engineers had not been built to withstand these unexpected forces and were damaged. Aqueducts designed by Roman engineers still bring water from the mountains to irrigate coastal fields today.

Roman aristocrats established huge estates, which they leased out to tenants who paid taxes and rent with grain that went to feed the Roman army. Tunisia became the "granary of the empire." The bulk of the population was still made up of Berbers who were assimilated into Roman culture. They farmed much of the coastal region, although slave labor was common also.

Merchants and craftspeople came to Tunisian cities from many parts of the Roman world. It was a cosmopolitan mix. Security was provided by Rome's frontier legions, who often stayed to claim land of their own as payment for past services.

## CHRISTIANITY IN TUNISIA

A growing number of Jews lived in Tunisia. They had been sent into exile after rebelling against Roman rule in Palestine during the first and second centuries A.D. Many of these Jews converted to Christianity. Carthage became the center of this new religion.

A scholar named Tertullian is regarded as the creator of Latin Christian literature. He was born in A.D. 150. Later St. Augustine, a native of Carthage, wrote his famous "City of God" passage. He preached the idea of a heavenly city whose citizens were temporary travelers in an earthly world.

For reasons that are not too clear, the North African people became passionately Christian and conversions were not always peaceful. There were more martyrs there than anywhere in the Roman Empire. Suicide was an acceptable way to prove one's Christian faith.

The *circumcelliones*, gangs of runaway slaves and dissatisfied peasants, tried to establish their own version of God's kingdom where all would be equal. Equality was often hurried along by robbery and murder.

The church was divided between Donatists and Roman Catholics. The Donatists represented an antiforeign nationalist movement. They wanted to appoint their own bishops without interference from Rome.

Although Donatism was officially classified as heresy, it was not defeated until the Vandals arrived from northern Europe.

# Chapter 4

# *VANDALS*

---

The Roman Empire in North Africa always had been thought to be impregnable. The sea protected the land from the north and the parched desert to the south, but it was too rich a prize to remain safe forever.

Hordes of Vandals from the area that is now Germany tried to attack Rome from the north. They almost succeeded, but the Roman army drove them off. The Vandals retreated but would not admit defeat. With more experience and better-trained troops, they found a way to attack the empire at its weakest point.

In A.D. 429 Geiseric, king of the Vandals, crossed over to the northern coast of Africa at the Strait of Gibraltar. He quickly overran Mauritania and Numidia to the west and laid waste to Roman and Christian civilization alike. He made the richest prize of all, Carthage, his capital. From his African base, he and his troops conquered Corsica and Sardinia.

The Vandals were Christians, as fanatic as the Donatists and just as opposed to the Roman church. In 455 Geiseric made his move on Rome again, carrying his standard, a Bible stuck on the end of a lance. The Vandals marched into Rome, stole everything they could carry, and sailed back to Carthage. The word vandalism, meaning destruction of property, comes from the name of these people.

For a century the Vandals ruled Tunisia. They changed their horsehair jackets and trousers for Roman togas and Carthaginian robes. They moved from tents into homes, but they left little of their own culture behind.

The Vandals tried to impose their religion by force. They were Arians, followers of the Alexandrian priest Arius, who denied that Christ was divine. The violence they used to rule their kingdom turned the people against them. The Berbers of Tunisia simply moved to the interior and kept their independence.

The Vandals remained an isolated warrior class, concerned with collecting taxes and exploiting the land they could control along the coast.

## WEARERS OF THE PURPLE

By the sixth century, the Roman Empire was gone. Rome was ruled by another tribe of barbarians from the north, the Goths. The Vandals were still in Africa; the Visigoths were in Spain.

A thousand miles (1,609 kilometers) to the east in Constantinople a Greek, who had become a Byzantine emperor and head of the Eastern Christian church, vowed to reunite the empire under his command. He was known as Justinian. He wrote a code of laws and built a magnificent church in Constantinople.

There was great pomp and circumstance in the church. Bishops wore cloaks of royal purple. Money and goods were taxed to maintain such elegance. Justinian sent his army abroad to spread his power. Little resistance was met until they came to Carthage.

In 534 Justinian's general, Belisarius, lay siege to the city. It fell in three months. Once more the Berbers, who had managed to survive under other regimes, continued their life-style with little

*St. Sophia, the magnificent church Justinian had built in Constantinople*

interruption. They simply moved inland and lived under their own tribal rule.

The Byzantine empire was centered in Constantinople, too far away to build a consolidated stronghold. Remains of walled towns and watchtowers along the coast show that it was not a peaceful rule.

Taxes were high, but not used to benefit those who paid the price. Under Byzantine rule the Roman engineering works were left to decay. No new roads were built. The water and irrigation systems were left in ruin. No form of political organization was developed to take the place of the orderly system the Romans had offered.

During the sixth and seventh centuries, the Byzantines and Persians, who lived farther east in what is now Iran, were constantly at war trying to bring nomadic tribes under their rule. It was a time when the people of Tunisia were looking for a leader, a crusade, to follow. It was to come in the form of a new religion from a distant place, the city of Mecca in the middle of the Arabian Peninsula.

# Chapter 5

# PRAISE ALLAH

Mecca had no government. It was controlled by a group of clans who paid tribute to the nomads who frequently attacked trading caravans crossing the Sahara desert. This guaranteed the safety of the caravans and gave traders a very good reason for routing their traffic through Mecca. Thus it was one of the wealthiest trading centers in the world.

It was already a holy site for Christians and Jews. Abraham is supposed to have built a temple in the shape of a cube in the middle of Mecca as thanks to God for deliverance from his wanderings. It had been rebuilt many times and was known as the *Ka'ab*, or cube.

There also were heathen idols that had been set up around the city to be worshiped by those who made the trip to Mecca.

Around 570 a child named Muhammad, meaning "he who is praised," was born in Mecca. He was orphaned at an early age and raised by an uncle. He never went to school, but his influence on the history of the world was to be great.

As a young man he found work as a camel boy with the caravans of a wealthy widow. He traveled widely and was able to explore the civilized world far from Arabia. When he was twenty-

*The Prophet Muhammad, as depicted by a non-Muslim. According to Islamic law, it is forbidden to draw a likeness of a person.*

five and his employer, the widow Khadija, was forty, they were married. He was considered a successful businessman living in modest luxury in Mecca. The couple had two daughters. Two sons died in infancy.

Muhammad, who had met Christians and Jews on his travels, realized there could be a more spiritual side to life than the materialism and trade that his Arabian family and friends seemed to worship.

He began to spend long hours in the desert contemplating what the future would bring. He had a vision, which he later said came from the angel Gabriel, who told him to go forth and spread the message of goodness and sharing. There was only one true God, Allah.

The religion he preached was called *Islam*, meaning "surrender" (to God's will), and his followers were *Muslims*.

He claimed no special powers, except through the revelations he received from God. He called himself the last of the "messengers," or prophets. He accepted Moses in the Old Testament of the Bible

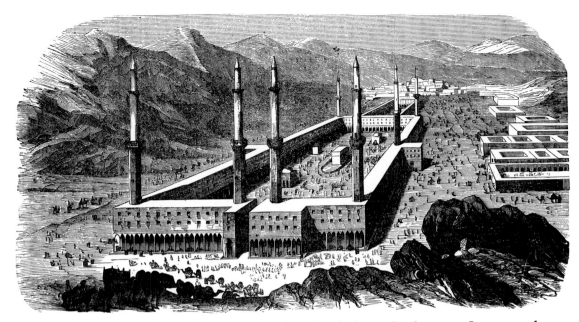

*The temple at Mecca*

as a prophet, and Jesus, too. But he did not look upon Jesus as the son of God as Christians do.

At first only a few people would listen to Muhammad's teachings. He told them that it was the obligation of wealthier Muslims to help the needy.

The tradespeople of Mecca did not like this philosophy. They also stood a chance of losing money if Arabs listened to Muhammad and stayed away from the holy city that collected fees for the right to worship in front of the 360 idols close to the Ka'ab.

After twelve years of harassment, Muhammad and his followers left Mecca and moved to Yathrib, a city 200 miles (322 kilometers) from Mecca. Inhabitants by the hundreds converted to Islam. The city of Yathrib was renamed Medinat Rasul-Allah (the city of the Apostle of God). It is now simply called Medina, the second-holiest city for Muslims after Mecca.

## YEAR ONE

The date of this migration, A.D. 622, became year one on the Islamic calendar. Eight years later Muhammad returned to Mecca and with an ax broke all the stone and wood idols in the city. He designated Mecca as the sacred city forbidden to all nonbelievers.

Before his death he set up a code of behavior similar to the Ten Commandments Moses had given to his people. Since Muhammad could not read or write, he committed them to memory and had his followers do likewise.

There are "Five Pillars" to the Muslim religion. One must swear to believe in God, Allah, and in Muhammad. Believers must pray five times daily facing Mecca. They must give alms to support the needy. To show their devotion, they must keep a month-long fast during the lunar month of Ramadan, and they must make a pilgrimage to Mecca at least once during their lifetime.

In 632, Muhammad died. The Muslim community appointed a committee of elders to select a replacement. Arab society has always revered age and experience. They selected Muhammad's father-in-law as the first elected caliph. He refused to be called a prophet. He felt his role was to lead the public prayers and interpret Muhammad's teachings.

The expansion of Islam beyond the borders of Arabia was swift. A green banner with a star and crescent was the symbol of the new faith.

## ISLAM AND THE BERBERS

By the time of the death of Prophet Muhammad in 632, most of the tribes in the Arabian Peninsula to the east had been converted to Islam. All others were considered infidels, nonbelievers, who must be brought by force, if necessary, to see the truth. Nomadic Arabs traveling west under the inspiration of their new religion were awed by the sophisticated cities they seized.

Arab armies met little resistance until they came to Tunisia. The Berbers again were ready to fight for independence, but in 670 the Arabs mustered all their forces to sweep into the country. Under their commander Uqba ben Nafi they founded a military base about 93 miles (150 kilometers) south of Carthage, which was still held by the Byzantines.

As the story goes, an Arab leader named Okba led his army on a long march into central Tunisia, away from the sea, to a wide flat plain bordered with salt marshes. Here he drove his lance into the ground and shouted, "I plant for Thee a Kairouan." *Kairouan* in Arabic means, "the place of arms." It was an armed camp, meant to be a base for Arabs to finish the conquest of North Africa. It is the oldest Muslim city in all Africa, founded three centuries before Cairo in Egypt.

## THE PRIESTESS

The Berbers would still not give up their independence. The leader of the resistance was said to be a woman. Her name was Kahina. She was a Berber, probably of the Jewish faith. Her name in Arabic means "priestess." She is supposed to have been able to predict the future. The Berbers trusted her.

When she realized that the Arabs had gathered such an overwhelming force that her troops were bound to be defeated, she ordered that their own crops and villages be burned. She fortified the old Roman colosseum at El Djem and rallied forces around her.

It was evident that they would not be able to withstand an attack. She ordered her three sons to surrender to the Arab general Hassan, then led her troops out of El Djem and into the

*An example of Moorish architecture*

mountains of Algeria. Much later—at the age of 127, it is said—she was finally killed, still fighting Arab forces.

Carthage fell in 693, but the last pockets of Byzantine resistance were not wiped out until the Arabs, masters of cavalry, obtained naval supremacy in the Mediterranean. They swept through Algeria and Morocco and in 712 invaded Spain. Within fifty years of their takeover of Tunisia they had conquered land on both sides of the Mediterranean. For a time North Africa and Spain shared a common culture and artistic legacy, which was called Moorish.

## A RELIGIOUS CENTER

Arab rule was not as harsh as might have been expected. The Arabs established their legal, social, and religious systems under a caliphate, the office of the prophet's successor. Arab Muslims did not persecute Christians or Jews. They were allowed to keep their faith and were exempt from military service if they paid a special tax, *jizya*, which was used to care for the poor.

*The Grand Mosque in Kairouan*

Tunisian towns prospered under Arabic patronage. Peace was restored. Arabs had come originally as conquerors and missionaries, not as colonists. They came without families and frequently married those they had come to conquer and settled to raise families.

Many Berbers found it to their advantage to convert to Islam, but they combined their new religion with their own folk religion. In the countryside Islamic scholars and teachers often were replaced by wandering holy men, *marabouts*, translated from *"al murabutim"* or *"those who have made a religious retreat."* They were seen as miracle workers. People turned to them for guidance as well as political leadership.

However, Tunisia came more directly under the orthodox influence of teachers from the religious centers of Tunis and Kairouan than other areas on the North African coast.

During the 800s Kairouan was a center of religious learning for all of the Maghrib region. Its scribes copied books in both Arabic and Hebrew. It was in large part through Arabic texts that classical Greek knowledge of medicine, natural science, and astronomy came to be recognized in Europe. Kairouan became a holy city of such importance that seven pilgrimages made there by a devout Muslim was equal in merit to the required trip to Mecca. Nine thousand worshipers have knelt at one time within the spacious courtyard and arched alcoves of Kairouan.

Although in the past the people of Tunisia had embraced Christianity with fervor, they now turned to Islam with equal enthusiasm. The Byzantines had made the church a complicated form to follow and an expensive religion to support. Under Islam, the poor were to be cared for. There were many who had suffered in the past.

Also there were strong ties between Arabs and Berbers, originating with their nomadic desert way of life. The problems that followed were caused by different sects of the Islamic religion, each trying to gain control of converts. Leaders proclaimed succession by birth.

## A FIGHT FOR CONTROL

The Shiites, sometimes called Fatimites because of their special loyalty to Fatima, daughter of Muhammad, were one warring group. Another were the Kharijite rebels, who believed in the equality of all Muslims. Three distinct classes had developed within the Islamic religion: Those who were direct descendants of Muhammad; those Arabs who had joined the movement after its return to Mecca; and last on the scale, the non-Arab converts to Islam, which took in most Tunisians.

Then there was Ibrahim el-Aghlab and his successors, who paid the caliph in Baghdad for the privilege of governing Tunisia. The

*An illustration shows St. Louis in chains after he was captured in the Seventh Crusade; he died during the Eighth Crusade.*

whole of the North African coast often was torn into small quarreling states, but the Aghlabid Dynasty did bring an era of prosperity. During some of the fiercest fighting, the magnificent holy city of Kairouan almost was destroyed.

## THE HAFSID DYNASTY

It was not until the Hafsid Dynasty was established that Tunisia had an organized government and religious security. Tunis was developed as the national capital. The Olive Mosque in Tunis contained a library of thirty-six thousand volumes, outshining the Grand Mosque of Kairouan, which had been considered the center of learning until armies laid it waste. Carthage, twelve miles (nineteen kilometers) to the north, developed into a luxurious suburb and busy seaport.

There was one moment in history when Tunisia felt the brunt of the religious crusades of medieval Europe. King Louis IX of France, better known as St. Louis, sailed for Tunis to conquer the city for Christ. He died of malaria and the crusade was a failure. Tunisia was given a breathing spell of peace.

*In 1453 the Turks conquered Constantinople.*

It was at this time that Tunisia began to engage more extensively in trade with Europe than the rest of North Africa. Treaties were signed with the Italian city-states of Genoa, Marseilles, Pisa, and Venice. There even were records of commerce with the king of Norway.

The Hafsids tried to bring about a peaceful coexistence between the unpredictable, independent Berbers of the interior and the ever-growing number of Christians coming from abroad. Their Muslim numbers were swelled by Spanish Muslims, or Andalusians, who were escaping from the Spanish reconquest, but world history again affected the future of Tunisia.

The Byzantine Empire in Constantinople collapsed under attack by Ottoman Muslim Turks in 1453. This shocked the Christian world and led European countries to consolidate their efforts to suppress Islam. In 1492 the Arab Muslims, who had built a stronghold of their culture and religion in Granada, Spain, were defeated and driven out of the country. The next century was to be filled with bitter rivalry between those carrying the banners of the crescent and those carrying the cross.

# Chapter 6

# BARBARY PIRATES

The capture of Constantinople ended the thousand-year-old Byzantine Empire. The Ottoman sultan, Mehmed "The Conqueror," established a Muslim Turkish kingdom. Later, in 1517, the Sultan Selim declared himself caliph as well. This made him, at least in theory, the commander of the faithful. However, it was a loose organization, the conquered and the conquerors each depending on each other.

The Arabs of North Africa found that their monopoly of the world trade routes had been usurped by the powerful city-states of Venice and Genoa. The Arabs found a very effective way to fight back. They resorted to piracy and retaliated by capturing whatever ships crossed their bows.

Their ships were fast, usually long and narrow, propelled by a crew of Christian slaves chained to banks of galley oars. A single slanted sail added to the ships' speed. The Arabs could dart out into the windward passage, overpower trading vessels, strip them of booty, and race back to safe anchorage on the Tunisian coast.

One form of booty angered Europeans. Captured crews were made slaves, frequently tortured, and chained to the oars of the galleys to help take another prize.

*Barbary pirates*

At first, attacks were unorganized, but the sultan of Turkey soon realized how easily he could put the pirates to his own use. He was without a navy to protect his Ottoman Empire, so he made deals with the Arabs. The Arabs could rule whatever towns they captured and keep all but one-fifth of their booty, their price for protection from land if Europe should send troops.

Very briefly the Spanish seized Tunis in 1573, but a renegade pirate recaptured the city in the name of Allah. He organized Tunisia with himself as regent in the name of the Ottoman sultan.

## THE REGENCY

The regency had three divisions of government: a *pasha*, directly responsible to the sultan; the *ivan*, or military council; and a *bey*, whose job it was to collect taxes, pay the troops, and supervise the administration of the state. It was not long before the bey became the real ruler of the country. It was a job to be coveted and one to be dreaded. Anyone with such absolute power and money at his disposal was fair game for assassination attempts. There were many plots and intrigues that led to bloodshed.

Stability came when a wise man, Husain Ibn Ali, realized that the only way to rule safely was to gain popular support from the people themselves. In turn, he guaranteed the people protection.

The Berber tribes for many years had obeyed only their chiefs and no one else. The beys imposed their authority by force, giving the nomads a choice of either settling in fortified and protected areas or migrating farther south in the desert area. Those who opted for freedom had their lands confiscated and then sold in large tracts to the beys and their supporters. In 1757 the Siali family received 1,350 square miles (3,497 square kilometers) of land near the city of Sfax. Gradually a new aristocracy developed around the bey and his extended family. Most were Turkish.

Tunisian development under the beys was unique for Arab land. The influence of the Ottoman sultan was slight. Trade treaties were signed by the bey of Tunis with many European countries. Again trade flourished.

The most significant accomplishment of the bey of Tunis was in the field of foreign relations when he outlawed piracy. Many other reforms were ordered, and a great deal was done to transform a traditional state into a modern one. Tunisia was considered far more civilized by European standards than the other Muslim countries of the North African coast.

If Tunisians had been left alone, they might have been able to hold their own against northern competition, but the nineteenth century was a time when the leading countries of the world, most notably France and England, were vying with each other for colonial empires.

# Chapter 7

# AS A FRENCH
# PROTECTORATE

By 1830 France had already taken over Algeria. In 1878 Great Britain agreed to a treaty allowing France a free hand in Tunisia in exchange for the leasehold on the island of Cyprus that the British had acquired from Turkey. This angered Italians, who considered Tunisia to be in their sphere of influence because of its close geographical location. But Italy was in no position to go to war with France over colonial rights. If they had, there might have been a very different chapter in Tunisian history.

The only excuse France had for invading Tunisian territory was ostensibly to pursue Khrumir tribespeople who had made raids across the border into Algeria. France sent a force of forty thousand, many more than were needed to subdue a few nomadic tribespeople.

French cavalry rode on to Tunis, while the French navy landed at Bizerte and occupied the port, which was far distant from the hills of the Khrumirs.

French officials met the governing bey at the Bardo Palace and presented him with a treaty giving the French military the right to occupy certain strategic posts temporarily to "keep the peace." The temporary visit lasted seventy-five years.

*Left: Al Sadok Bey*
*Right: French*
*troops demanded*
*the surrender*
*of Kairouan.*

Al Sadok Bey signed the treaty on the condition that the troops would not enter Tunis. Once the Khrumirs were defeated and some of the French troops began to pull out, the bey denounced the treaty and sent word to Turkey that he expected protection. The French immediately returned and occupied the country.

New provisions of the treaty were enforced, which gave the French an active role in government. Officially the government that had been set up under Turkish rule three hundred years before was to be kept intact. The bey continued to appoint a cabinet, but its members had to be approved by the French resident general, and all business passed by the cabinet had to be approved by officials who reported directly to Paris.

The Tunisian court system was reformed under the French system. Tunisia's foreign debt was consolidated in a single 125-million-franc loan from France. Suddenly a system of buying and selling, profit and loss, was substituted for the old tradition of barter. French became the official language, though few Tunisians spoke French.

Tunisians, as well as all French citizens living in Tunisia, were conscripted into military service. Prior to World War I, the French Foreign Legion stationed more than twenty-five thousand soldiers within the country.

## WHO OWNS WHAT?

The hardest system to reform was the ownership of property. The traditional concept outside of the cities had been that land belonged to the tribe. There were no definite boundaries. They could shift as frequently as the weather.

Another complicated form of land tenure before the French arrived was called the *habus*. It meant dedicating the revenues of property for a charitable purpose, usually in the hands of the Islamic hierarchy. This kept estates from being subdivided among quarreling heirs or being confiscated by the government. The land was still used by the original owners and their descendants who paid a small yearly rent to the religious institution.

Sweeping changes were made as the French simply ignored previous land titles. In 1885 a Land Registration Act was passed. All land titles were placed before a council. European colonists flocked to Tunisia to bid on unclaimed land.

In the past, land had meant wealth. Now wealth was measured by the produce the land earned. The Tunisian farmer with his donkey and plow was no match for the European farmer with machines. The only hope for survival for many was the life of a sharecropper, or *kammas*, an Arabic word denoting the one-fifth of the crop a sharecropper received for working the land.

In defense of the French system, it could be pointed out that schools were built, lighting and telephone systems installed, and

*The French-built commuter train between Carthage and Tunis is still in use today.*

paved roads extended throughout the countryside. New
government buildings went up, making Tunis look like a carbon
copy of Marseilles, the French port across the Mediterranean.

Railroads were built and an electric suburban train connecting
Tunis, Carthage, and Garmath offered good service. It is still in
use today. An important boost to the economy came with the
development of phosphate mines for the manufacture of
fertilizers, which were exported throughout the world. The typical
Tunisian farmer could not afford fertilizers.

There was an invisible line between the measured success of the
Tunisian citizen and his French counterpart. Skilled craftspeople
could not compete with manufactured goods brought in from
France. Business management jobs and professional services were
monopolized by the French.

A slow ferment of dissatisfaction began to build. It started in the
very classrooms the French had built to teach the glories of French

history, the history that told about their own fight for equality.

## FIGHT FOR EQUALITY

World War I had little effect on Tunisia, although sentiments against colonization were openly expressed when the peace treaty was being drafted. Tunisians only could hope that the Fourteen Points put forth by United States President Woodrow Wilson would soon receive worldwide acceptance. The Twelfth Point said that all subject peoples under the old Ottoman Empire should have the right to manage their own affairs.

A group called the Young Tunisians started printing their own newspaper demanding a free Tunisia. One of the leaders of the group, Sheikh Taalbi, wrote a book that was widely distributed. His own set of demands included a new bill of rights for his people, a new land registration system recognizing all Tunisian claims, and an economic development plan that would benefit all citizens, not just a few. The book was widely read and the Destour party was founded on these principles.

For fourteen years the Destour party kept the hopes of the Tunisian nationalist movement alive. A few reforms were brought about, but those who were impatient for more change felt their leaders had sold out too soon. The leaders of the Destour party were the elite, well educated, and wealthy of the country. They also were conservative, represented by old men in flowing robes.

Some of the younger middle-class Tunisians were looking at alternative forms of government. Socialism and Communism, unheard of before, now were being considered. They were searching for a more aggressive leader. The young middle class found him in Habib Bourguiba.

# Chapter 8

# HABIB BOURGUIBA

Habib Bourguiba was born in 1903 in Monastir, one of the oldest towns along the coast. His father had been an officer in the bey's army, but his grandfather had taken part in a major uprising against taxes imposed by the old bey's regime. Habib was the youngest of seven children. His mother died when he was four. Bourguiba was sent to Tunis to live with one of his brothers, who was active in the Young Tunisian movement.

Bourguiba attended the university in Tunis and went to Paris to study law. He returned home in 1927 with a French wife and a young son. He immediately became active in politics.

He questioned the workings of the government. Why was garbage picked up in the European section of Tunis, but not in the medina where most Tunisians lived? Why were lights installed along the streets where the wealthy French lived but not in the medina? Tunisians as well as the French were being taxed for these services.

The final break with the government came when it was announced that Tunisians, who had become French citizens to take their share of some of the French benefits, could not be buried in Muslim cemeteries. The Destour leaders said nothing.

*German tanks in Tunis in 1943 (left) and the port city of Sousse in 1945 (right) after the Germans and Italians had been driven out*

The Bourguiba followers called for a party congress to organize their complaints. No one from the old Destour group came.

The Neo-Destour group was founded, with Bourguiba as secretary-general. It was not a political party as is known today, because political parties were not allowed during the French Protectorate. But, point by point, Bourguiba bargained for reform. It was the old Arab form of barter. Bourguiba often compromised but never surrendered. The movement was led by a group of militants who frequently were thrown in jail for their efforts. Bourguiba himself spent more than half of the next twenty years in jail separated from family and friends.

## WORLD WAR II

During World War II, Tunisia became a strategic goal for both sides to conquer. The French already had troops along the North African coast, too close to the heel of Italy for the comfort of Benito Mussolini and Adolf Hitler.

*General Leclarc (left)*
*and Habib Bourguiba (right)*

The German and Italian forces arrived by air from Sicily to wipe out the Allied troops. Nearly fifty thousand landed on Tunisian soil and engaged in some of the bitterest fighting of the war. The Free French forces under General Leclerc, as well as New Zealand and Indian troops, fought alongside the British and Americans. Fields around Bizerte and Cap Bon are still littered with leftover shells and equipment from the battles.

Bourguiba spent most of the war in a French prison for having incited rebellion with his fiery words. In 1942 after France was overrun by Germans, he was freed by the Nazis. The Italians put a palace at his disposal, hoping to use him to swing Tunisians over to the Axis side.

In February 1943 the Germans attacked Sidi Bou Said and the Kasserine Pass, but failed to make gains. The weather had turned the desert into mud. Tanks were bogged down. By May 13 the German force was surrounded and defeated.

Bourguiba had always had confidence that the Allies would win. Now he felt the time had come to press forward for a free Tunisia, but the French were not ready to surrender their claim.

*Bourguiba is welcomed home in 1955.*

## HELP FROM ABROAD

Meanwhile Bourguiba was seeking international support for his cause. At the end of World War II he had secretly gone to Egypt. In the spring of 1949 he went to Paris, and the following year to the United States, India, Pakistan, and Indonesia. His love of his country kept him from settling in safer surroundings.

He returned home with a list of seven demands. The seventh point demanded an elected Parliament that would write a constitution. Again he was arrested and put in jail in France. From his cell he kept up a correspondence with other leaders of the nationalist movement.

A change of French policy came in 1954. A new French premier, Pierre Mendes-France, proclaimed the self government of Tunisia on July 31, 1954. Home rule was still not independence, but it was the first promising break Tunisia had. Bourguiba was released and returned home to a hero's welcome in Tunis.

The French military remained in Tunisia and controlled the police. It was not until June 1, 1956, that the Tunisians could fly their red flag with its white star and crescent over the Bardo Palace.

## Chapter 9

# TUNISIA FOR TUNISIANS

Bourguiba was the unanimous choice for president of the new republic. The constitution gave him vast powers. He was able to issue laws and decrees with legal force. He could appoint his own cabinet and he was head of the armed forces.

He preached that Tunisians needed to take pride in their country and learn dignity for themselves by improving their standard of living. Part of this could be accomplished through education. Dozens of new schools were built, but as the French moved out there was a severe shortage of teachers. Still it was a step in the right direction.

Bourguiba's next goal was to provide jobs for the needy and to improve health care. It was a tremendous task, but he had the support of the whole country.

Without denying Islamic faith, polygamy, the right of a believer to have as many as four wives, was banned. Women were given equal rights with men. Women from the countryside frequently continued to hide their faces behind veils, but their daughters adopted Western customs.

Thousands of children who had wandered the streets of the cities as beggars were housed in "Bourguiba Villages," where they were taught reading, writing, and useful trades.

The country was making great strides toward modernization, but Bourguiba was not happy that a large group of French military still were based in Bizerte. In 1961 Tunisian troops blockaded the French naval base, and heavy fighting broke out. Over a thousand French soldiers were killed before the French agreed to evacuate the base. The last French forces left in 1963. The following year Bourguiba expropriated the lands owned by all foreign settlers. Landless peasants were settled on the old French estates. Through cooperatives, they shared the profits of the farms.

## POLITICS

The president's hold on power was absolute. There was only one legal political party between 1963 and 1981, the *Parti Socialiste Destourien* (PSD). In 1974 the constitution was altered to allow Bourguiba to become president for life. He also was allowed to confirm the prime minister, who was then Hedi Nourira, as his successor. It was not until July 1981 that the *Parti Communiste Tunisien* (PCT) was recognized. President Bourguiba then announced that any party that had obtained 5 percent of votes cast in legislative elections also would be recognized.

Finally relations between the Maghrib countries improved. A long-running border dispute with Algeria was settled, and a final agreement with Libya was reached over the rights of Tunisia to drill for oil under the sea in the Gulf of Gabes.

Diplomatic relations between the two countries had been strained when Libya expelled some thirty thousand workers who were Tunisian citizens. Tunisia, in turn, charged Libya with spying. Now the rift was mended, at least in writing, but not all problems were solved so promptly.

*In 1974 Colonel Moammar al-Qaddafi of Libya and President Bourguiba signed a treaty to merge their nations, but the merger didn't last.*

In October of 1985, relations with the United States were strained following the bombing of the temporary headquarters of the Palestinian Liberation Organization (PLO) near Tunis by Israeli planes. Seventy-two people, including twelve Tunisian citizens, were killed. The United States government at first publicly supported the right of Israelis to conduct the raid in retaliation for the murder of Israeli citizens in Cyprus by the PLO. Later diplomatic apologies were exchanged.

## PRICES SOAR

In 1984 the cost of food soared. A drought had damaged crops. The price of bread rose 115 percent. People rioted in the streets and troops were sent in to quiet them. More than a hundred people were killed. An official inquiry into the disaster blamed the minister of the interior for failing to notify the president about the seriousness of the situation. He was accused of trying to bring about a crisis for his own political gain and to discredit Bourguiba. Bourguiba immediately cut prices of staple food items and fired the accused minister.

49

The following year there was a series of demonstrations by students and Islamic militants over low wage scales, union rights, and lax religious laws. Bourguiba had tried to do away with fasting during the month of Ramadan. The devout had always followed the law of the Koran, their Bible. They were not supposed to eat or drink from sunup to sundown for one whole month. They made up for it by feasting and celebrating all through the night. Because of this, not much business was conducted at this time of the year. To stay in competition with Western countries, Bourguiba tried to stop these practices, but he was criticized by many of the more conservative Muslims.

Those who opposed him went through the countryside trying to stir up trouble. A series of strikes was called. A group of religious extremists backed by the Iranian government brought terrorism to the streets of Tunis. In March 1987, Tunisia severed diplomatic relations with Iran. Members of radical Islamic groups were arrested for treason. Ninety defendants were brought to trial and sentenced to death.

Ben Ali, who had been appointed prime minister and secretary-general of the PSD, urged Bourguiba to show restraint. Bourguiba became so angry that he fired his cabinet and replaced them with inexperienced men who had no knowledge of running the government. Bourguiba's orders changed from day to day; there was chaos.

On November 7, 1987, seven doctors declared that President Bourguiba was unfit to govern because of senility and poor health. Prime Minister Zine el-Abidine Ben Ali was sworn in as president. He immediately announced that reforms would be made. The party's name was changed to the *Rassemblement Constitutionnel Democratique* (RCD).

*Zine el-Abidine Ben Ali,
prime minister and
president*

A series of proposals was presented to the National Assembly. The constitution was rewritten to abolish the post of president for life. The term of office was limited to five years, and no person could assume office past the age of seventy. Bourguiba had been eighty-four at the time he was removed from office.

The constitution provided that the president, as the head of state, was to appoint a Council of Ministers. The prime minister would be directly responsible to the president. For local administration, the country was divided into eighteen governorates, giving the local population a much more active role in self-government.

Tunisia has come a long way in a very short period of time, entering the often confusing stage of European competition without relinquishing her past heritage and Islamic faith. Habib Bourguiba had been the one to lead the country in a bloodless revolution. His name will always be remembered. His successors are finding ways to combine democracy with a strong head of state.

*An old section of Tunis*

# *Chapter 10*

# CITIES AND VILLAGES

What is Tunisia like today? It is still a land of contrasts. City life and country life are as different as living in the twentieth century and living during biblical days. There are luxury homes and apartments in the capital city of Tunis and elegant hotels along the coast, yet there are places in the south of Tunisia where, for generations, people have dug their homes into the ground.

## TUNIS

Even in Tunis you will see two distinct areas of the city, the old and the new. Tunis is built upon low, chalk-white hills that step down toward a salt lake, El Bahira, near the harbor. The Lake of Tunis was once a shallow lagoon hemmed in from the Mediterranean by a long sand spit.

However even in Phoenician days, sailors had made a passage so they could use the area as a safe harbor. It wasn't until 1893 that the French cut a twenty-foot (six-meter) channel across it to develop the port of Tunis. A dike on either side keeps water from water.

A four-lane highway and an electrical rail line are built along this artificial barrier. The little white train that heads north to the

*A panorama of modern Tunis (left); Avenue Habib Bourguiba (right)*

beach resorts was brought to Tunis in 1890 from Paris. It was considered too outdated for the French capital, but today serves passengers very well, skimming across the water, it seems, at moderate speeds.

The skyline of Tunis is blocked in squares by modern buildings, domed here and there by mosques and spiked with minarets, while loaf-shaped roofs scallop the poorer sections. The square tower of the Great Mosque rises above the heart of the city. The Great Mosque of Ez Zitouna is both a place of worship and a famous university founded in 732. Its name means "The Olive Tree," so called because its founder taught his disciples under the shade of just such a tree on this very site more than twelve hundred years ago.

*Above:* Bab el-Bahar,
*the ancient entrance
to the medina
Left: A Muslim
scholar studying
in the Great Mosque
of Ez Zitouna*

In medieval times the sea came up to the entrance gate of the walled city. New Tunis has been built in part on reclaimed land. The broad Avenue Habib Bourguiba, lined with Barbary fig trees, leads straight up to the *Bab el-Bahar* (Sea Gate).

The old section, the medina, is still threaded by a maze of alleyways that lead away from a great Roman arch into the *souk*, or bazaar. Here the passageways are roofed over with tin or brick or sometimes only straw mats to make them into vaulted tunnels. The vast souk is partitioned off like sections of a beehive, each craft having its own allotted place.

Its shadows are alive with sounds of the hammering of copper, the thudding of rugs being tossed in heaps for display to shoppers,

*Many things are available in the hubbub of the Tunis medina including leather goods (left) and copper articles (right).*

the slapping of hands against the bellies of jars, and the bray of donkeys. Guttural voices, often interrupted by the whine of strange music, issue from radios at full blast. Skewers filled with mutton crackle over flames. Coffee and mint tea steep in metal pots over samovars that keep the water hot with glowing charcoal nuggets. And then there are the perfume shops and jasmine vendors to sweeten it all.

Bargaining is a way of life. A buyer should never believe a merchant who starts the selling process by saying this is the lowest price possible. It is a game of wits to be played, and rarely won.

Tunisians can brag there is little crime in their country, possibly because punishment is severe.

*Clothing and beautiful rugs also are found in the market.*

Older men in their white *jibbahs*, bathrobe-style coverings with a hood, and tasseled red skullcaps are sipping their coffee, while older Muslim women scuttle through the corridors enveloped in white *sifsaris*, cloaks or wraparound shawls, their faces no longer concealed behind black silk. This is as far as they have wanted to go in their emancipation. However many of today's generation are wearing the latest in Paris fashions. Some wear miniskirts, while grandmother keeps her head modestly covered.

Businesspeople in Tunis usually speak French. Arabic is the language of the masses, with few, a very few, remembering the language of the Berbers. Five times a day worshipers are called to prayer. "*Allah Akbar*," which means "God is most great!" is chanted by a keeper of the faith from atop the city's minarets. In some cases today's words are taped and magnified by electronic

*A minaret (left); the Bardo Palace (above)*

devices, but always there is a *muezzin*, similar to a priest, to put the process in motion.

In the mosques worshipers remove their shoes and wash their feet in a pool for that purpose. For those who must say their prayers close to their work or their home, a prayer rug is unrolled and they bow facing the holy city of Mecca. Schoolchildren in their smock uniforms are doing exactly what their parents are doing at the same moment. As testimony to their total submission, part of the prayer is said with the head touching the ground, the body always facing the holy city of Mecca to the east. True Muslims refuse alcohol and eat no pork. Friday is their sacred day.

In many Islamic countries nonbelievers are not welcomed at mosques, but Tunisian mosques are open to visitors, except when prayers are being said.

The present Bardo Palace was built in 1882 on the site that had once been the headquarters for the beys' Ottoman regime. It now houses Parliament and the National Museum. The Bardo Museum

*Left: Habib Bourguiba Avenue, the major boulevard of Tunis  Right: The city maintains an efficient bus system.*

is known throughout the world as the warehouse of some of Rome's and Carthage's most beautiful artwork.

Many of the mosaics that once floored villas and public forums of Carthage and the prosperous port of Tabarka are now laid out for visitors to see, to touch, even to walk upon. They were stripped from their original sites for safekeeping. Owners of some of the most humble farmhouses at one time paved their sheep pens with the priceless stones or sold them to more knowing collectors. There is a trend now to return them to their origins, restore them, and guard them for future generations.

Surrounding Tunis are areas of makeshift shanties, *gourbis*, where families, whose lives had once depended on following flocks of animals, have settled. Gourbis are really a permanent form of tent. Hundreds of nomads have flocked to the city in search of jobs. It is a problem still to be solved.

A few miles from downtown Tunis is the Belvedere, a green park on the highest of the city's hills. It was once a royal park.

Now it is home for the affluent. There is an Olympic-size swimming pool, a tennis club, a gambling casino, and a Hilton Hotel.

## CARTHAGE

Heading north from Tunis are the grisly sites of the Phoenician temples of Tanit and Baal Hammon, where children were sacrificed to the gods. The Punic port of Carthage lies ahead. At one time, before the age of landfill, it is said the harbor could shelter 220 vessels.

Carthage itself, the once noble center of North African civilization, has little to show for its past. It is now a commuters' suburb for Tunis, a role that was once reversed. The Baths of Antonius still are impressive. They were built during the reign of Hadrian in the second century A.D. What is left today is merely the basement structure, with stores of oil for the furnaces and earthenware pipes for the hot water they supplied. One of the Corinthian columns that once supported the roof weighs 4 tons (3,629 kilograms).

There are also ruins of the Martyrs Amphitheater where many a Christian lost his life. The present monument to Christianity was built by a Catholic missionary order, called the White Fathers. They built two lavish cathedrals, one in Tunis and one in Carthage. Since many of the French who supported the church have moved away, mass is said to only a few, but the schools and agricultural experimental stations the priests developed have made a lasting impression on the country.

One of the five palaces once occupied by Bourguiba is on the outskirts of Carthage. It is a low, sprawling building with many

*Ruins (above) of the Baths of Antonius, built by the Romans, and part of modern Carthage (below)*

*Left: A typical blue door decorated with square black nails   Right: The port of Sidi Bou Said*

arches and heavy wrought-iron chandeliers. Much of the work of governing Tunisia is still carried on in this residence, for it is the tradition of Arab rulers that the president be available to meet his public for all sorts of personal problems at the *dívan,* or audience.

## SIDI BOU SAID

Sidi Bou Said is just beyond Carthage. Here the coast juts out of the sea in a high promontory, and the view is magnificent. For centuries it has been a sentry post. In peacetime, bonfires burned as beacons to guide sailors.

The road to Sidi Bou Said turns and twists, becoming a narrow cobblestone track between white walls that hide the living quarters and gardens of many artists and writers who have made this a unique cultural as well as tourist center. Blue doors spiked with large square black nails in geometric patterns block entrances. The clear blue water below the cliff is dotted with pleasure boats.

*Left: Decorative iron grills are used to cover windows.*
*Right: The port of Bizerte*

## BIZERTE

In contrast, Bizerte is the country's busiest commercial port. It is a city with an ancient history all its own, but its historical monuments have not been groomed for the tourist. Bizerte is a working port. It is a deep-water harbor where during World War II submerged submarines could slip in and hide.

There are 125 acres (51 hectares) of docks accessible to the largest warships and commerical tankers. There are four dry docks, one nearly 1,000-feet (305-meters) long, that can handle repairs on ships from all nations.

## TABARKA

Continuing west along the north coast of Tunisia, close to the Algerian border, is another busy port, Tabarka. At one time wild animals from Africa were shipped from here to supply the

*Cork trees (left) and a tailor at work on the street in El Djem (right)*

gladiator games and Christian sacrifices in ancient Rome. Now bales of cork are on the docks ready for shipment around the world.

There is a strong smell of burned cork around the various processing stations where smaller chips of the valuable wood bark are dried, ground, and pressed into sheets of corkboard for insulation and manufacture into a number of products.

The countryside around the city is lush and green, with steep mountains as a backdrop to the sea.

## DOUGGA AND EL DJEM

Heading away from the coast, there are two ancient cities that are so well preserved it is like walking back in time. Across a plain of wheat fields and olive groves and past a ridge of hills is Dougga. The stone columns of the original city look down from its hillside over the long Numidian highway still rutted by chariot

*The colosseum at El Djem*

wheels. Three temples stand guard over its empty gateway. There was the forum, the slave market, the baths, and an amphitheater seating some six thousand.

This is dwarfed by the colosseum at El Djem with its three tiers of high arcades that could hold an audience of sixty thousand. It is the third-largest colosseum of the ancient world and has stood the test of time better than the one in Rome. Excavations are still unearthing prizes that tell us the luxury of life during the time of the Roman occupation.

## KAIROUAN

Kairouan is the center of Islamic history. The Great Mosque was originally built in 695, extended in 743, rebuilt in 774, and rebuilt again in 836. It is the oldest mosque in North Africa. It was built to hold the precious library of Islamic, Greek, and Arabic literature.

*A forest of columns in the prayer hall of the Great Mosque at Kairouan*

Its domes are shaped like closed tulips. A look inside the Great Mosque is like looking into the heart of a forest, whose trees are made up of 414 columns of marble, granite, and porphyry of every color to support arches that form seventeen naves. Nine thousand worshipers have knelt there at once.

The floors are covered with handsome carpets donated by the faithful who make the holy pilgrimage to Kairouan. It may seem strange to see crudely chiseled Christian fish symbols on some stone steps, but the conquerors built this mosque from stones stripped from monuments to older religions. The columns are of Roman and Byzantine origin.

The wealth of other countries is exhibited in Venetian chandeliers and panels carved in Mesopotamia from Greek marble. Baghdad provided tiles and Byzantine mosaics of lapis lazuli.

*Above: A carpet merchant chats with a customer in his shop.*
*Left: Women in the old section of Kairouan*

To the European and American tourist, Kairouan is best known for its exquisite carpets. They are works of art that take months to complete. Individual sellers carry them on their backs to display to the visiting buyer. More prosperous middleman merchants have showrooms where the wealth of color and pattern is piled high. Knowledgeable buyers, particularly from the Middle East, buy carpets as a cash investment, keep them protected in bank vaults, and use them as collateral for loans to carry on other business transactions. They have found that a Kairouan carpet has a constant or increasing value — a hedge against inflation.

## HAMMAMET AND SOUSSE

Along the coastline of Tunisia that faces east, there are a series of resort towns that boast the most modern hotels. Hammamet is

Cities on the east coast:
Monastir (above), Sousse (right),
and Hammamet (below)

a twelfth-century frontier town that is a working fishing village and can boast of a turreted Spanish battlement, but its main industry is tourism. A perfect climate and near-endless beaches have brought thousands of vacationers.

The broad beaches of Sousse have filled up rapidly with glass and stucco hotels in the past few years, but it also has an industrial side where Tunisia's first automobile assembly plant is located.

## MONASTIR

The next coastal town is Monastir, out on the promontory that marks the end of the Gulf of Hammamet. It began as a Phoenician settlement, later served as the base for Caesar's African campaign, and now has become famous as the birthplace of Habib Bourguiba.

## SFAX

On the way south to Sfax, it is easy to guess its most important export product. Olive trees fill up the plain that surrounds the city. They are planted in straight intersecting rows, each tree seventy-five feet (twenty-two meters) from its neighbor. The trees, some of which could be a thousand years old, have gnarled trunks and heavy crowns of gray-green foliage. During harvesttime the long branches bow low toward the ground. The mills that press the oil are sometimes as old as the trees.

Knowing how important their treasure is to the country, the people of Sfax have become very independent and it is a closed society that has maintained its own aristocracy by intermarrying

*An ancient
fishing village
on the Gulf
of Tunis*

among the families with the most wealth. They have been able to
fight many of the Socialist ideas of the government because their
knowledge and experience brings wealth in the form of taxes to
the government.

Modern Sfax is a city of wide streets, fronted by houses of a
pink hue that are decorated with graceful iron grillwork. There is
also an old section, the medina, where many of the old Sfax
aristocracy prefer to live in their ancestral Arab homes.

## THE SEA AND THE SHORE

Traveling south from Sfax, the land turns dry and dusty. It is
not yet the land of the Sahara, but profit now comes from the sea.
It is an excellent commercial fishing ground for tuna, mackerel,
and sardines. Even youngsters without a boat can bring in a
sizable catch by luring fish into their nets.

The youngsters wade out into the surf holding a line to which is attached a full-size sea bass, perhaps 15 or 20 inches (38 or 50 centimeters) long. This live decoy attracts others of its kind and when a dark shape swirls in with the waves, the fisherman throws his weighted circular net. In other protected coves where the water is deeper, swimmers with masks and flippers surface with all kinds of weird sea life on their spears.

The sea itself looks like a giant dye pot stirred with every shade of blue from aqua to indigo. The water is such a vivid blue, one feels a body would be forever stained that hue. Yet splashing the surface, the color fades to transparency and the swaying rocks thirty feet (nine meters) below seem touchable.

## DJERBA

The most popular tourist island off the coast of Tunisia is the "Land of the Lotus Eaters" of *Odyssey* fame from the writings of the Greek poet, Homer. According to legend, when Ulysses landed on the enchanted island of Djerba, a strange madness took over the crew. One bite of the local lotus blossom and all desire for family and country disappeared. They had only one thought—to stay forever on the beautiful island. Ulysses had to bring them back to the boat by force and tie them with chains to continue his voyage.

Some might still agree that even today Djerba has a powerful effect over tourist and native alike. No one wants to leave. The island has a near-perfect climate. It is surrounded by crystal-clear water and white sand beaches.

The island is a flat plot of land with little vegetation except palm and olive trees and hedges of Barbary fig. Beautiful hotel accommodations are available. The houses of the natives all seem

*The town square of Djerba*

alike, small white cubes with walls of limestone. The roofs are
made of split palm trunks or arched vaults of cone-shaped brick,
looking like little helmets.

Djerba is an island of considerable size, about eighteen miles
(twenty-nine kilometers) in each direction. There is an airport and
a number of small villages. Sorting fact from fiction, it is certain
that Djerba was an important Phoenician trading post. In later
history Arabs brought with them a new religion and a new
language. Djerba embraced the Muslim faith, but founded a sect of

*The castle at
Houmt Souk (above),
the capital
of Djerba,
and a stretch
of beach (left)*

its own that has remained independent of some of the beliefs of
the mainland.

There are two Jewish communities in Djerba, Hara Kabira and
Hara Srira. It is generally recognized that the synagogue at Hara
Srira, called La Ghriba, was built some six hundred years before
the birth of Christ. Legend has it that it was built around a sacred
stone that fell out of the sky. A mysterious foreign girl, a *ghriba*,
helped the builders with miracles and gave the place its name.
Djerba has long been considered a magical place.

*Above: Gardens (left)
and a general
view of Gabes (right)
Below: Workers
restoring a ghorfa*

# Chapter 11

# A DESERT LAND

Gabes is the most southern seaport of Tunisia. Although it is located on the Mediterranean, it is an oasis city and is known as the "Gateway to the Desert." From the desert plateau that surrounds the city, a river of green can be seen. But if one steps back a few paces, only the barren sweep of sand and rock remains visible.

Gabes has 300,000 date palms, as well as olives, bananas, oranges, pomegranates, and vegetables growing in a deep canyon. It is a strange sight to see such a contrast of geography and vegetation in one small area.

About fifty miles (eighty kilometers) inland is a fringe of unique Berber villages in an arid moonscape setting. Medenine is made up of two separate parts, a relatively modern village with administration buildings and the traditional trading center.

Many years ago Berbers built strange "skyscraper" complexes, some as high as five stories. They are barrel vaulted and windowless, one piled haphazardly on top of another. These houses are called *ghorfas* and are reached by mud stairs or ladders. They were probably built as fortified granaries and places to hide in times of trouble. The builders pressed the images of hands and feet on the ceilings to protect them from evil spirits. Not many are lived in these days, but are used for grain storage.

*Underground houses in Matmata*

Even stranger houses can be found in Matmata. People live at the bottom of enormous holes dug more than twenty feet (six meters) into the ground. On approaching the settlement, all that can be seen are spirals of smoke rising from the ground.

To visit one of these strange houses one walks down steps or a ramp dug from the dirt into a large square courtyard open to the sky. Living rooms, bedrooms, and storerooms are hollowed out on the sides of the courtyard. Even the beds are made of mud, on which sheepskins and blankets are piled. Baskets, pots, pans, and other utensils are hung easily on the mud walls. For centuries these people of the desert have found an efficient way to keep cool in the summer and snug in winter.

## A LAKE IN THE DESERT

South of the Dorsale Mountains and north of the Sahara's waterless wastes is a huge shallow salt lake, Chott el Djerid. At

*Chott el Djerid, Tunisia's largest salt lake*

times this 70-mile (113-kilometer) depression in the ground loses most of its water, becoming a nearly dry salt plain.

There are a number of smaller chotts in the area, which at one time must have been part of the Gulf of Gabes. Long ago they were cut off by drifting sands from the Mediterranean. Chott el Djerid is by far the largest. Since it is below sea level, all the moisture that does fall on this barren land drains into this depression.

Engineers and dreamers have been trying for years to alter the climate of the desert. One ambitious plan would be to cut canals to drain water from the Mediterranean into these saltwater chotts. They speculate that a whole new climate might develop. The theory is that breezes from the Sahara blowing across this water would be cooled and pick up moisture that might drop as rain on the surrounding land. But the chance that this desert will become green is far into the future.

More practical solutions may come with the hope of tapping large reservoirs of water buried under the Sahara desert. Wells have been drilled in some places. Data from orbiting satellites in outer space have shown rock formations long since covered by sand that lead geologists to believe they were old riverbeds. They think that the water has simply filtered into the ground and could someday be pumped to the surface.

These projects would take millions and millions of dollars, something a small country like Tunisia does not have, but someday the world may need more land upon which to grow crops. The Sahara desert covers about one-fourth of all Africa and only a small portion lies within the boundaries of Tunisia. So these dreamers are not giving up their hopes for greener fields.

## OASES

The land can be coaxed to grow crops when water is available. At Tozeur natural springs are directed into ditches to irrigate date palm groves. The trees stand tall and arch over the sky, making a cathedral roof of slotted palm fronds. In spring peach, apricot, almond, and plum trees are in bloom, giving a profusion of scents that seem strange in a land surrounded by mountains of sand.

The homes of Tozeur are famous for their intricate patterns of brickwork. People have been living here for centuries. There are camels and donkeys for transportation, but no sheep. The land produces other wealth.

Nefta, Tozeur's nearest neighbor, has 350,000 date palms and 152 springs that bubble water to the surface. Irrigation tunnels, instead of open ditches, channel the precious water to small fields. If the water were left uncovered, the intense heat would evaporate the moisture before it reached the fields.

Few mechanical pumps exist. Animal and boy power bring the water to the surface. A young boy leads a camel, harnessed to a wheel, around in a circle. The water drains into the tunnels that eventually moisten the edges of crop rows.

*In the middle of the harsh, dry desert, an oasis provides welcome refreshment.*

In the oases there are rigid systems of water and land use. Water rights are auctioned off each year. The highest bidders keep enough water for their own crops and resell the surplus. Individual landowners are responsible for maintaining their sections of the irrigation system.

In a few areas, the government has spent funds to drill deep wells. The garden patches here are farmed as cooperatives, the growers receiving a percentage of the harvest.

Nefta was once a very important stop on the caravan route through the desert, the last stop before the blazing journey across the Sahara. It has been kept alive by a 2,137-foot (651-meter) well drilled in the 1960s. The government in Tunis has been trying to interest foreign capital investments in similar projects, but the chance of earning profits has to be calculated in future years.

# Chapter 12

# NATURAL RESOURCES

Unlike its Arab neighbors, Tunisia has not been blessed with oil wealth. Geologists are still drilling in the hopes that they will reach the enormous reserves that are found in Algeria and Libya, its next-door neighbors. So far only limited quantities have been discovered. In some ways this has given Tunisians a more stable economy because they have been forced to develop other resources. The prosperity of the country is not tied to the world market price of oil.

There are some natural gas wells at Cap Bon. Also some low-grade coal of poor burning quality has been found in the area. This supplies Tunis with domestic needs, but other cities depend on imports.

Tunisia's mineral resources are limited. In the far northwest, near the Algerian border, there are some iron ore deposits. All mines are open pit. The ore is high grade, but the supply is limited. At one time production was exported, but beginning in the 1970s production was deliberately cut back to reserve the ore for a growing domestic steel industry.

All minerals are state owned, although contracts with private companies are made to explore new deposits.

The one outstanding natural resource is phosphate rock from which agricultural fertilizer is made. Tunisia ranks fourth in the

*Plowing farmland with camel power*

world production of phosphates. However the quality of Tunisian phosphate rock is lower than that of competitors, and mining costs are higher.

More workers are hired by the government than are actually needed for an efficient operation. This practice was started as a means of giving employment to the poor in the south of the country where no other means of support was available. The government is trying to make the industry a profitable one by developing more valuable by-products of phosphate.

## AGRICULTURE

Agriculture still provides the income to support about one-half the population. Of the arable land, only about one-fifth is under cultivation. The rest is pastureland where sheep and camels are the most common domesticated animals.

*Almond trees bloom among cacti (above);
harvesting dates at the top of a tree (right)*

The principal cash crops are wheat, barley, oats, corn, sorghum, citrus fruit, grapes for wine, and olives. Figs, pears, apricots, apples, plums, cherries, and almonds are other crops that earn income for the economy. Experimental farms near Tabarka are trying to improve production.

Because of the long growing season in Tunisia, there are many fairly large vegetable farms along the northern coastal region. Beans, artichokes, turnips, eggplants, peppers, potatoes, and peas are grown for export. Canning plants have been set up with government funds to accommodate surpluses.

Because of the climate and soil conditions, most of the wheat is of the hard shell variety, which when milled yields semolina, good for the production of pastas such as spaghetti, and used in one of the most popular types of dishes Tunisians love, called *couscous*. Soft grain wheat to make bread must be imported.

82

*Left: Olive presses are used to extract olive oil.*
*Above: An olive grove*

The olive tree is well suited to the Tunisian climate because it can survive long periods of drought. Production varies widely from year to year depending upon rainfall and care. Seldom are there two good years in a row.

Tunisian olive oil has long been known as Tunisian "gold." The government has tried to reduce the number of olive trees, while improving the productivity of those that remain. Some families own only a single tree and that one might be hundreds of years old. It is hard to convince them to cut down such a veteran and plant a new one that may take years to mature.

Date production is important to the people living in the southern region. Sometimes during drought years, this may be almost the only food available in the desert area.

Before the French arrived in numbers in the 1800s, only small areas of land were planted with grapes, wine being forbidden to Muslims. French farmers planted vineyards. For many years wine was exported to France. Today the market for this product has dropped, and the land is being replanted with other crops.

*After cork is stripped from the trees, it is neatly piled and taken to a processing center.*

The government is experimenting with sugar beets to cut down on the necessity of importing this commodity. Fields of cotton also are being planted to provide for an enlarging textile industry.

Esparto grass, which grows wild in the steppe, is gathered for the manufacture of paper and rope.

Another crop that has been harvested for centuries is cork. Cork comes from the outer part of the bark of the cork oak. The cork is first removed when the tree is twenty years old. As this first layer is rough and has deep furrows, it is not very valuable. It is shredded and used in insulation board, floor tiles, table mats, and other products.

After the first stripping, the cork is removed from the tree every ten years or so. First it is seasoned by being exposed to the open air. The rough outer part is then scraped off, the rest flattened and dried.

Tree felling for firewood and charcoal and clearing land for agriculture have severely depleted timber reserves and have left the hills of the highlands of the country bare and susceptible to erosion. The government has plans to stop this. Nearly 400,000 saplings have been planted each year. It is hoped that within fifty years the young forests will change the whole picture of the landscape in the high country, but there is no way they can coax trees to take hold in the desert.

## COOPERATIVES

In 1967, 92 percent of all farmland in the country was managed as cooperatives, meaning the land was owned by the government. Farmers were paid in wages or produce for working the farms. It was thought this was the only way to increase production—by using state funds to furnish modern machinery and to pay for fertilizer and irrigation projects.

Many private farmers objected. Physical violence erupted in many areas. Police backed by army units were forced to step in to bring peace. During the two-year period of forced cooperatives, farm production fell. Many officials who were put in charge of projects had no agricultural training whatever.

Bourguiba was wise enough to admit the policy had been a failure. By 1970 the government shifted from a controlled economy to a more free-market economy. Farmers were given the option of remaining with the cooperatives or returning to private ownership.

The government still tries to control some long-range planning through education. Many farmers depend on a single crop— wheat. They are urged to diversify, plant more than one crop, so

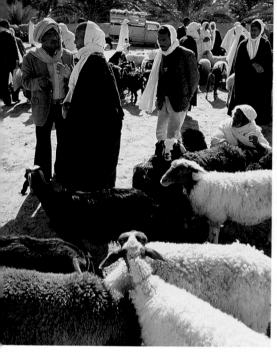

*Above: Commercial fishing boats in Bizerte*
*Left: Sheep and goats at a livestock market in Duz*

that their whole livelihood is not based on the price of one commodity or the whim of the weather.

Although some dairy cows are raised in the north, sheep and goats are the predominant livestock raised in Tunisia. Most farmers or nomads tend to let their stock graze on marginal government-owned land. When drought cuts back on pasture, animals are either left to die in the fields or brought in for slaughter well before time.

The government is now urging farmers to cultivate fodder for their flocks. Breeding stock is being imported, but the country has a shortage of veterinarians to carry on these projects. In a land where herders have always been at the bottom of the social scale, it is hard to get professionals to enter this field.

## FROM THE SEA

An estimated twenty thousand Tunisians earn their living from fishing. A government-financed program is trying to help fishermen buy new boats. In turn, the government owns part of the trawler fleet. There have been few complaints. The average income of fishermen has increased with the use of new equipment.

There is an abundance of fish off the Tunisian coast, enough so that a limited number of Italian fishermen also are allowed to fish in coastal waters in exchange for an annual payment.

## FOREIGN INVESTMENT

From the beginning, Bourguiba realized that foreign investment in Tunisia was the only way to accumulate enough cash to carry out his long-term goals for modernizing the country. When Tunisia first became a Socialist country, all foreign-owned land was taken over by the government. This definitely discouraged any further commitments by citizens of other countries to invest capital in Tunisia.

In 1972 Tunisia was the first country to sign a World Bank International Investment Arbitration Agreement, which set up specific rules on how foreign investors would be paid for their services and their property, if at any future time the government would decide to nationalize these industries. This lessened the fears of foreign capitalists and led the way for many large projects.

Tourism has become a very profitable industry. One had only to look across to the other shore of the Mediterranean to see how many people flocked to the shores of France, Italy, and Greece. Tunisia had a sunnier climate, miles of sugar-white sandy beaches, and more historical monuments than could be found in any country twice its size.

The only thing lacking was hotels to tempt travelers. Several international hotel chains had shown interest, but guarantees had

*A luxury hotel on the island of Djerba modeled after the local architecture*

to be met that the profits these investments would make would not be confiscated by the government. Once this international investment agreement was made, the door was open for progress.

Today the number of luxury hotels is growing. Africa's largest hotel, the 2,450-bed Dar Jerba, is located on the island of Djerba. It is a handsome, low, spreading complex, complementing the local architecture with its arches and domes.

Once tourists started to come, money was spent on many services. Even the most humble craftsperson has found an expanded market for his produce. The farmer sells more food staples, and the government-owned airline and transportation services find business good.

The government has been trying also to interest foreign manufacturers to produce their goods in a country where there is an ample supply of workers. True, the labor force is unskilled but anxious to learn.

The government has offered tax incentives for foreign investors to build their factories away from the capital city of Tunis. They are trying to create jobs for the poor, who have been flocking to the city in search of work. This has helped spread employment opportunities through other parts of the country.

Today automobiles are being assembled in Tunisia. Household appliances are manufactured in factories, in contrast to the small one-family operations of the past. There is a growing textile and leather industry and shoes are being exported.

## HOME INDUSTRIES

The government has helped find foreign markets for traditional home industries. Tunisia has long been noted for its beautiful crafts, which are really works of art. Fine carpets from Kairouan and Gafsa have been treasured since they were first transported by camel caravans across the Sahara or across the sea by early sailing ships.

They are still handwoven on ancient looms in traditional patterns of bright blues and reds. Children are trained at an early age to knot individual strands of wool to the warp of the loom. After each knot the yarn is cut and beaten down in an even line. When a row is completed, the wool is again brushed and clipped to a firm depth of pile, all this while following exactly a pattern of dots in front of them. Large carpets may take several years to complete, but the life of such a carpet is almost forever. Antique rugs several hundred years old are still in use.

Nabeul is the center of the pottery industry. Potters work from certain basic designs, yet each piece is slightly different from all the others. The potter squats before a heavily weighted wheel,

*Mosaics, here shown on the roof of the Grand Mosque in Tunis (above), are a centuries-old Tunisian craft; pottery from Nabeul (above right); the delicate wire bird cages (right) of Sidi Bou Said*

which he spins with his toe. A single ball of clay suddenly springs to life through the pressures of his fingers and becomes either a long-necked jar, cup, bowl, or serving dish. When it is lifted from the wheel, it is set aside to dry for a day or two before another craftsperson traces a delicate glazed design with a paintbrush. The product is finally fired in a large oven, or kiln, before it is a finished product. Some of the pots are covered with a stretched ox hide to make a drum, or *darbukas*.

Mosaics are still a part of Tunisian artistic culture. Contemporary artists have used this centuries-old craft to decorate the walls and floors of public buildings. Another architectural addition to the homes of the wealthy are intricate wrought-iron grills at the windows. Windows are never screened and only shuttered when the weather turns cold.

*An artisan decorating
a copper vase (above);
handwoven rugs (right)*

Metalworkers of Tunisia have been shaping copper into all sorts of useful and decorative products over the years. Other home industries include leather goods and olive-wood utensils. Sidi Bou Said is famous for its delicately worked wire bird cages of blue and white.

The chief shopping area of city and rural areas alike is the souk. The city souk is open every day, except religious holidays, from dawn until noon, closing down for a two-hour lunch break and continuing until sundown when there is another call to prayer. In the country the marketplace is usually open once a week. Souk al Arba, for example, translates literally to Market of the Fourth (Day), Wednesday.

Retailers in the big souks are organized into guilds managed by an official who collects rents and acts as mediator in all disputes.

# Chapter 13

# WAY OF LIFE

---

**HOUSING**

The growth of the Tunisian economy is impressive when measured against other developing countries. One of the major factors has been political stability.

Tunisia has associated herself with European countries as much as her Arab neighbors. Surprisingly enough, she even urged the Arab world to acknowledge Israel's existence in an effort to bring peace to the Middle East. Tunisia is respected by other Arab states and is the headquarters for the Arab league. The PLO has its official headquarters near Tunis.

While other Arab states have poured millions of their oil wealth into investments abroad, Tunisia has been guarding her income for undertakings in her own country: road building, irrigation projects, and construction of homes for the needy.

There has been a great need for more housing in the cities. This was caused by several factors. Since Tunisia became an independent nation, there has been a growing middle class of shopkeepers, bureaucrats, and teachers. When private housing owned by foreigners was taken over by the government, a large number of residential properties were left vacant until this newly created class of Tunisian nationalists moved in.

SOCIÉTÉ DE PROMOTION DES LOGEMENTS SOCIAUX

CONSTRUCTION
DE 450 APPARTEMENTS

*Although they are not popular with Tunisians, government apartment buildings help ease the need for housing.*

However working-class housing was scarce. Country people were moving to the cities in great numbers, especially to Tunis. The newcomers either camped out in squatters' hovels in the outskirts of town, or tried to squeeze into the older section of town in the medina.

Once-elegant mansions of the early Turks were turned into tenements where a whole family might share a single room. The sewage system originally designed for a population of forty thousand was called upon to serve four or five times that number.

Young couples, who in the past might have continued to live with parents, now wanted homes of their own. Higher standards of living called for better housing than the mud huts of an earlier generation. The government stepped in to help in the crisis. Some apartment houses were built, but they were not popular with either the new or old generation. People wanted traditional housing.

*In many urban residential areas, front doors open directly onto the street (left). A low wall encloses a house, with a typical loaf-shaped roof, on the island of Djerba (right).*

Except for the villas of the wealthy, most homes are small and built of stone, concrete, or adobe, because there is so little lumber available. In the cities where people have crowded close together, neighboring walls touch each other, and front doors open directly onto the streets. With almost no windows, light and air enter through narrow interior courtyards. Although small in number of square feet at foundation level, houses expand with vertical space, often having two or three stories with an outdoor living space on the roof. There is an almost universal color scheme—white walls and blue doors. Some say blue is the magical color that blesses the family.

In the country almost all houses are enclosed with a low wall meant to keep out stray animals and also to keep the wind from blowing away the family garden or covering it with shifting sand.

Without lumber to make strong overhead beams, there is only one way to roof a house of brick. Early builders learned how to slant bricks in an arch, wedged against each other with a keystone in the center. That's why there are such graceful loaf-shaped, or domed, houses in this part of the world.

Furnishings are sparse, but often lovely carpets grace dirt or stone floors or are piled on benches to be spread out for company. Most kitchens seem primitive with only a single burner fueled by charcoal. An oven is often a brick cubbyhole in the wall. Refrigeration is provided only in newer city dwellings.

Few have water within the house, because wells have to be dug so deep. A whole community shares the water. It is not unusual for families to have to haul their drinking and cooking supply long distances. Land close to the well can be irrigated for crops and is too valuable to be used for homesites.

These farmhouses are lavish in comparison to the way the nomads live. Everything the nomads own is worn on their backs or can be strapped to the carrying saddles of their camels. Often rugs, blankets, and a cooking pot or two is all they have.

Their tents are large and low, but whole families live in this cramped space. The tents are usually made of matted (felt) wool, which is excellent insulation against heat, cold, and wind.

## FOOD

Delicious meals are prepared in these simple kitchens and outside fires. Tunisian cooking is hearty and spicy with traces of French and Indian influences.

Throughout the Maghrib region the most popular dish is couscous. To prepare this dish, semolina wheat is sprinkled with oil and water, rolled into tiny morsels, steamed, and then covered with a thick, hot tomato sauce and whatever happens to be available: fish, beef, mutton, or vegetables.

*A* brik *stuffed with seafood*

To add to the spiciness, almost every Tunisian table offers a supply of *harissa,* a condiment of ground red pepper, garlic, and oil, which is guaranteed to burn the tongue of the uninitiated. Couscous is regularly served both for lunch and dinner, accompanied by fruit in homes where families can afford the luxury or can grow their own.

*Chakachouka* is a salad so popular that it is simply referred to as "salade tunisienne." It is made of tomatoes, onions, peppers, and hard-boiled eggs.

A Tunisian version of a thin pancake is called a *brik.* It is fried in hot oil and stuffed with meat, eggs, or spinach. Vendors in the souk or on street corners do a brisk business selling briks.

Several types of cheese are produced by the government-owned dairy, the most popular being *numidia,* a blue cheese. Goat milk provides several varieties of tangy cheese. Butter is rarely used.

The country's choice of beverage is either strong Turkish coffee or a very sweet mint tea. Some people add to the flavor by putting

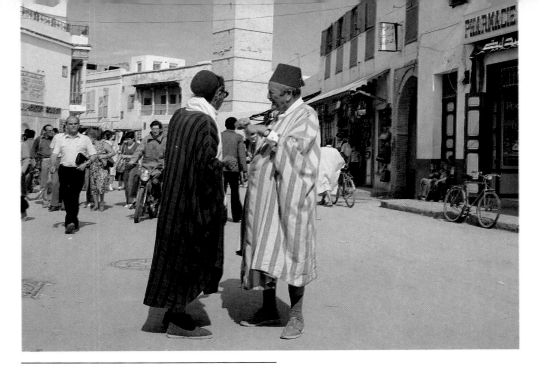

*Men wearing traditional* chehias *and* djellabas

big chunks of cube sugar in their mouths and noisily straining the tea through their teeth. This is not considered at all impolite.

In cities and in resort hotels, almost any kind of food is available, European or American style. A bargain for tourists is the African lobster, which is brought live to the table for selection. All kinds of seafood and shellfish are available along the coast, usually as fresh as the morning catch.

## DRESS

Most Tunisian businessmen wear Western suits, but they often add a *chehia* on their head. This is a type of fez, brimless, tall or pillbox, round or flattop, brown or red, depending on the part of the country they come from.

The more traditional costume for men is the *djellaba*, a short-sleeved tunic reaching to the ankles. In the true desert, these robes are much larger—the *gandourah*—loose bat-winged garments with

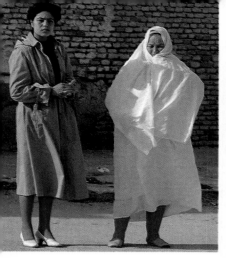

*Above: One woman is wearing Western clothes while her companion wears a* sifsari. *The country woman in the center is dressed in a* mellia *and a* futa. *The Berber woman (far right) has tattooed her face.*

cowl-shaped hoods that protect the wearer from sand, wind, heat, or cold.

Women's garments vary much more with the region. In Tunis European dress is most common, but the sifsari is still frequently worn as on outer garment over Western-style dress. Its loose folds are used to carry packages, even babies, and it still can be used as a veil when pulled together in front of the wearer's mouth and held in place with her teeth.

Veils were rarely worn by country women because they would have been a nuisance working in the fields. The traditional fashion is the mellia, a loose drape like a sari, worn in combination with another drape across the shoulders called the *futa*. This is fixed to the mellia with large silver pins or a belt wound at the waist.

Berber women have been wearing makeup for centuries. It is common for them to outline their eyes with a black substance, *kohl*. Some faces are tattooed with ocher and blue dots. For special occasions designs are painted on hands with henna dye, which lasts on the skin for several weeks.

The women frequently wear handsome jewelry of silver, copper, brass, and sometimes gold. Turquoise and amber, a form of petrified resin from trees that once grew in this arid country, are both supposed to have magical protective powers for the person wearing them.

In the old days banking was a novelty. Jewelry adorning rural women represented family savings. These adornments always have value and can still be traded for livestock or other essentials. They are now collectors' items, often sold to tourists in the souks.

## THE TUNISIAN PEOPLE

Over 50 percent of the population of Tunisia is under twenty years of age and 70 percent live in the Tell and Sahil regions. With better government-sponsored health care, the aging population is bound to increase. The country is in a state of change, but the single most important factor influencing the social values of the country is the religious background of Islam.

The very harshness of the climate has strengthened this belief. Drought, pestilence, and other misfortunes are thought to be caused by the will of God.

It is common for towns to have patron saints. The word *sidi* means saint in Arabic. Thus the towns of Sidi Bou Said and Sidi Daoud are named for holy people.

Because it is God's will, no Muslim should be ashamed of being poor. A person in need can expect assistance from neighbors as well as relatives. Old and disabled were automatically cared for in the past.

*Tunisian faces reflect the traits of the many invaders over the years.*

The accumulation of wealth has never been considered a top priority, except to provide modest comfort. In the traditional culture of the cities, the pursuit of scholarly activities is more highly valued than wealth and status.

Peasants and nomads, on the other hand, were traditionally suspicious of city values. Book learning did not teach survival in the harsh realities of day-to-day living. So again Tunisia is a land of contrasts.

The United States has often been called the melting pot of immigrating cultures. Tunisia, with its much longer history, is indeed a blend of the many invading people that have fought their way across the country. Phoenician, Greek, Roman, Vandal, Byzantine, Arab, Turkish, and French people have all added their traits to the original Berber stock to produce the modern Tunisian.

In appearance Tunisians come in all skin shades, from the olive-skinned Mediterranean type to the black skin of sub-Saharan African races, whose ancestors were brought in as slaves.

Two minority groups who have guarded their origins are the Jews and the French. The latter group arrived from France after the establishment of the French Protectorate in 1881, but there are many more Jews in the country than Christians. The Jewish community is concentrated in Tunis, with smaller colonies in Sfax and the island of Djerba. There were three distinct times in history marked by the migration of Jews to Tunisia: those who came here from Palestine after their city of Jerusalem was burned by Roman Emperor Titus, those who were finally expelled from Spain by King Philip III in 1610, and the middle class of tradespeople who came from Europe in modern times.

Not only are Tunisian Jews full citizens, but they have never suffered the persecution and intolerance that Jews experienced in Europe. Many Jewish Tunisians were strong supporters of the nationalist movement in the struggle for freedom from France. They have often held high posts in the Tunisian government.

One of Tunisia's finest writers is a Jew, Albert Memmi, whose semiautobiographical novel, *The Pillar of Salt*, tells of Jewish family life in the cities of Tunisia.

## THE FRENCH INFLUENCE

Although the French now make up only a small portion of the population, they have stamped their lasting influence in many ways. The architecture of government buildings and homes of the wealthy marks the time the French were in charge. Even the layout of the wide boulevards with traffic circles in Tunis and Sfax is very much a French conception. The narrow streets of the medina left no place for socializing. The French also built parks and sidewalk cafés.

*Long loaves of crusty bread and sidewalk cafés are part of Tunisia's French inheritance.*

The French brought with them their two-hour lunch habit and their five-to-seven break for wine or tea. They insisted on French bread. Tunisians still bake the long loaves as well as the flat crusty bread of the Arabs.

The French influence on the politics and economy of the country is still felt. Tunisia needs to export to the European Economic Community, which provides an important market for Tunisian exports. At the same time, Tunisia is increasing its ties with its Arab neighbors.

## EDUCATION

The Tunisian school system was adapted from the French model of education. There are six years of primary schooling, followed by three more of secondary classes. During the next three years, students are required to specialize their academic interests while some select vocational training.

*Schoolchildren in Carthage*

Students who survived rigorous tests and were permitted to continue in college were thought to have the best chance for higher paying jobs. However in some cases the drive for formal education has succeeded too well. There are not enough nonscientific jobs to go around. There are too many language scholars, lawyers, and social scientists. Today those with technical skills, who know how to install plumbing or how to operate machinery, have their pick of jobs.

Tunisia has its own university founded in 1960 to replace an Institute of Higher Studies that was organized by the French in 1945. The current enrollment is approximately thirty thousand students. Two new universities were opened in 1986 at Monastir and Sfax.

Laws passed in 1958 made public education free at all levels and available to all regardless of race, sex, or religion. However there are no rules that say school attendance is mandatory.

As late as 1953 only 12 percent of Tunisian children were in

*Signs outside the entrance to Belvedere College are in French and Arabic.*

school, and these were almost all boys. Fathers did not think it important that girls be educated, but today's statistics show that 77 percent of all children attend. Girls make up half the classes in the cities. In the rural areas girls are still frequently tied to household tasks.

The government is urging adults, who never had a chance to learn to read or write, to go to school. Adult illiteracy is dropping—in the 1980s by 20 percent. However there is still 45 percent of the total population who cannot pass the tests.

Most classes are conducted both in French and Arabic, but classes are being switched to Arabic as much as possible. It is a trend meant to unify the country, to give more equal opportunities to the poorer classes, who know only their native Arabic language.

In 1988 the government spent 14.6 percent of its total budget on education. That is a record that few, if any, countries can match.

One remaining link to the past is the *kouttab,* or grammar school, taught by religious scholars. These schools are discouraged by the present government as being archaic, not allowing young people to become part of the modern world. The pupils sit cross-legged on mats facing the master, who guides the chanting until he is satisfied they have committed all 114 passages from the Koran to memory.

But whether children take formal religious training or not, most families insist on traditional acceptance of the Muslim faith. That still includes prayer five times a day. Family authority is apt to be stricter than in Western culture. Mothers generally rule the home during a child's early life, but the father's word is law on major issues.

## WOMEN'S ROLE

Women have been starting to exert their rights. Careers come with education, but tradition is hard to break. Few women wear veils their ancestors were required to don. Yet many women cover their heads in public with simple scarves as a social reminder of the past.

Certainly in urban areas, marriage is a decision made by both men and women, yet there is little dating among teenagers until they are ready for marriage. Until they enter the university, boys and girls attend separate classes.

## LANGUAGE

Arabic is the language of all Arab countries from Morocco in the west to Iraq in the east, but there are such varieties of accents

*Arabic and French signs at the train station in Tunis*

it is hard for travelers across borders to understand each other. Even within Tunisia there are different dialects, although the coming of state-owned television and radio broadcasts has helped to standardize the spoken language.

Arabic is written from left to right. The letters are all curves and scrolls, beautiful to look at. Frequently ornamental script is included in works of art.

Very few people understand the original Berber tongue. Only about 1 percent of the population speak Berber as their first language. French, of course, is still the important language for international trade and foreign diplomacy. Two of Tunis's four daily newspapers are printed in French. English, German, and Swedish are often understood in port cities and resort areas.

## MUSIC

There is a type of music, *malouf*, heard only in Tunisia. It is a complex interweaving of sound on lute and guitar. Frequently the

*The Tunis Symphony Orchestra (above)
and desert musicians (right)*

players sing along with the melody. These are sad songs. Listeners are often moved to tears, which proves to the performers they are applauded.

The origin of this style is somewhat of a mystery, but it is thought that the Arabs brought their music to Spain in the eighth century, blended it with Iberian folk songs of the area, and reexported it to Tunisia in the seventeenth century when all Jews and Muslims were driven from Spain.

## THE FUTURE

Young Tunisians have cast their lot firmly for modernization, yet they have not forgotten their Islamic background. They are being trained to meet the challenges of a changing world, and are taking the best of each heritage.

Habib Bourguiba, the real creator of modern Tunisia, once said, "Tunisia is a young country with an old heart."

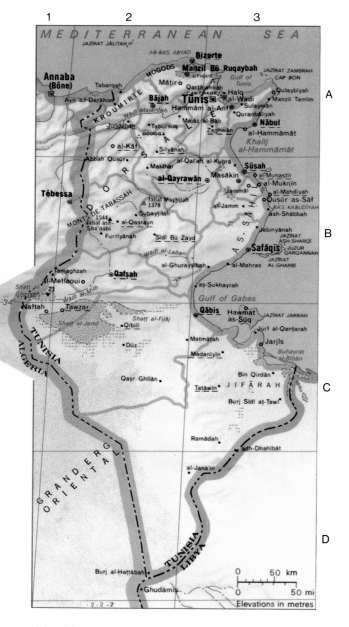

## MAP KEY

| | | | | |
|---|---|---|---|---|
| Abbah Qusur | B2 | | Majaz al-Bab | A2 |
| Abyad, ar-Ra's, *cape* | A2 | | Makthar | B2 |
| Ayn ad-Darahim | A2 | | Manzil Bu Ruqaybah | A2 |
| Bajah | A2 | | Manzil Tamin | A3 |
| Biban, Buhayrat al-, *lagoon* | C3 | | Masakin | B3 |
| Bin Qirdan | C3 | | Matir | A2 |
| Bizerte | A2 | | Matmata, see Matmatah | C2 |
| Bon, Cap, *cape* | A3 | | Matmatah (Matmata) | C2 |
| Burj Sidi at-Tawi | C3 | | Medenine, see Madaniyin | C3 |
| Carthage, *ruins* | A3 | | Mediterranean Sea | A1, A2, A3, |
| Carthage, see Qartajannah | A3 | | | B3, C3 |
| Dhahibat, adh- | C3 | | Metlaoui, al- | B1 |
| Djem, El, see Jamm, al- | B3 | | Milh, Wadi al-, *watercourse* | B2 |
| Djerba, Ile de, see Jarbah, | | | Mogods, *mountains* | A2 |
|   Jazirat, *island* | C3 | | Monastir, see Munastir, al- | B3 |
| Djerid, Chott el, see Jarid, | | | Muknin, al- | B3 |
|   Shatt al-, *salt marsh* | C2 | | Munastir, al- (Monastir) | B3 |
| Dorsale, *mountains* | A2, A3, B2 | | Nabeul, see Nabul | A3 |
| Dougga, *ruins* | A2 | | Nabul (Nabeul) | A3 |
| Duz | C2 | | Naftah (Nefta) | C1 |
| Fijaj, Shatt al-, *salt marsh* | C2 | | Nefta, see Naftah | C1 |
| Furriyanah | B2 | | Qabis (Gabes) | C3 |
| Gabes, Gulf of | B3, C3 | | Qafsah | B2 |
| Gabes, see Qabis | C3 | | Qal'ah al-Kubra, al- | B3 |
| Gharbi, Jazirat al-, *island* | B3 | | Qarqannah, Juzur, *islands* | B3 |
| Gharsah, Shatt al-, *salt marsh* | B1 | | Qartajannah (Carthage) | A3 |
| Ghurayyibah, al- | B3 | | Qasr Ghilan | C2 |
| Halq al-Wadi | A3 | | Qasrayn, al- (Kasserine) | B2 |
| Hammam al-Anf | A3 | | Qayrawan, al- (Kairouan) | B3 |
| Hammamat, Khalij al-, *gulf* | A3 | | Qibili (Kebili) | C2 |
| Hammamet, see Hammanat, al- | A3 | | Qulaybiyah | A3 |
| Hammanat, al- (Hammamet) | A3 | | Quranbaliyan | A3 |
| Hattabah, Burj al- | C2 | | Qusur as-Saf | B3 |
| Hawmat as-Suq (Houmt Souk) | C3 | | Ramadah | C3 |
| Houmt Souk, see Hawmat as-Suq | C3 | | Safaqis (Sfax) | B3 |
| Jabinyanah | B3 | | Sfax, see Safaqis | B3 |
| Jalitah, Jazirat, *island* | A2 | | Sha'nabi, Jabal ash-, *mountain* | B2 |
| Jamm, al- (Djem, El) | B3 | | Shabbah, ash- | B3 |
| Jammal | B3 | | Sharqi, Jazirat ash-, *island* | B3 |
| Jana'in, al- | D3 | | Sidi Bou Said, see Sidi Bu Zayd | B2 |
| Jarbah, Jazirat (Djerba, Ile de), | | | Sidi Bu Zayd (Sidi Bou Said) | B2 |
|   *island* | C3 | | Silyanah | A2 |
| Jarid, Shatt al- (Djerid, Chott el), | | | Sousse, see Susah | B3 |
|   *salt marsh* | C2 | | Subaytilah | B2 |
| Jarjis | C3 | | Sukhayrah, as- | B3 |
| Jundubah | A2 | | Sulayman | A3 |
| Jurf al-Qantarah | C3 | | Susah (Sousse) | B3 |
| Kabudiyah, Ra's, *cape* | B3 | | Tabarka, see Tabarqah | A2 |
| Kaf, al- | A2 | | Tabarqah (Tabarka) | A2 |
| Kairouan, see Qayrawan, al- | B3 | | Tabassah, Monts de, *mountains* | B2 |
| Kasserine, see Qasrayn, al- | B2 | | Tabursuq | A2 |
| Kebili, see Qibili | C2 | | Tamaghzah | B1 |
| Kroumirie, *mountains* | A2 | | Tatawin | C3 |
| Laban, Wadi al-, *watercourse* | B2 | | Tawzar (Tozeur) | C2 |
| Madaniyin (Medenine) | C3 | | Tozeur, see Tawzar | C2 |
| Maghilah, Jabal, *mountain* | B2 | | Tunis | A3 |
| Mahdiyah, al- | B3 | | Tunis, Gulf of | A3 |
| Mahras, al- | B3 | | Utique, *ruins* | A3 |
| Majardah, Wadi, *river* | A2 | | Zaghwan | A3 |
| | | | Zambrah, Jazirat, *island* | A3 |

# MINI-FACTS AT A GLANCE

## GENERAL INFORMATION

**Official Name:** Republic of Tunisia

**Capital:** Tunis

**Official Language:** Arabic. French is taught to all schoolchildren and is commonly used in administration and commerce. Small numbers of people speak Berber.

**Government:** Tunisia is a republic. Its 1959 constitution puts legislative power in the Chamber of Deputies, which consists of 136 members serving five-year terms. Executive power, however, rests in the president. The president is assisted by a cabinet that he appoints and that is headed by a prime minister.
The Destourian (Constitutional) Socialist party has been the dominant, and often the only, officially recognized party since independence.
There is an independent judiciary headed by the Court of Cassation; the president appoints its judges.

**Religion:** Virtually all Tunisians are Muslims. Tunisia has a small French community who are Roman Catholic, however, and about 9,000 Sephardic Jews.

**Flag:** Centered on a red ground is a white disk bearing a red crescent and a red five-pointed star.

**National Anthem:** "Al-Khaladi" ("The Glorious")

**Money:** The Tunisian unit of currency is the dinar. In 1989, one dinar was worth 1.2763 U.S. dollars.

**Weights and Measures:** Tunisia uses the metric system.

**Population:** 6,966,173 (1984 census); 7,362,000 (1987 estimate); 53 percent urban, 47 percent rural

**Cities:**

Tunis . . . . . . . . . . . . . . . . . . . . . . . . . . . . . . . . . . . . . . . . . . . . 596,694
Sfax . . . . . . . . . . . . . . . . . . . . . . . . . . . . . . . . . . . . . . . . . . . . 231,911
Ariana . . . . . . . . . . . . . . . . . . . . . . . . . . . . . . . . . . . . . . . . . . .  98,655
Bizerte . . . . . . . . . . . . . . . . . . . . . . . . . . . . . . . . . . . . . . . . . .  94,509
Gabes . . . . . . . . . . . . . . . . . . . . . . . . . . . . . . . . . . . . . . . . . . .  92,258
Sousse . . . . . . . . . . . . . . . . . . . . . . . . . . . . . . . . . . . . . . . . . .  83,509

(Population based on 1984 census.)

## GEOGRAPHY

**Highest Point:** Jabal Shanabi, 5,066 ft. (1,544 m)

**Lowest Point:** Chott el Rharsa, 76 ft. (23 m) below sea level

**Rivers:** The Majardah, the most important river system, rises in Algeria and drains into the Gulf of Tunis.

**Mountains:** Several ranges of the Atlas Mountains extend into Tunisia from Algeria. The Tunisian branch is called the Tunisian Dorsale chain.

**Climate:** Northern Tunisia has a Mediterranean climate with hot dry summers and mild rainy winters. At Tunis the average monthly temperatures vary from 48° F. (8.8° C) in January to 79° F. (26° C) in August. The Atlas ranges are cooler. The broad plain of central Tunisia has a semiarid steppe climate ranging from about 50° F. (10° C) in winter to over 80° F. (26.6° C) in summer.

**Greatest Distances:** North to south: 485 mi. (781 km)
East to west: 235 mi. (378 km)

**Area:** 63,170 sq. mi. (163,610 km²)

# NATURE

**Trees:** There are a great variety of trees, including cork, oak, pine, jujube, and gum. The mountains are covered by forests of juniper, laurel, and myrtle. Olive trees are prominent in the south. Esparto grass, the characteristic vegetation of the steppe region, covers over one-fourth of the country.

**Animals:** Jackal, wild boar, and several types of gazelle are numerous. A species of wild sheep called the moufflon is found in the mountains.

# EVERYDAY LIFE

**Food:** Tunisian cooking is hearty and spicy with French influences. *Couscous* is the most popular dish. It is made of semolina wheat rolled into tiny morsels, steamed, covered with a hot tomato sauce, and used with fish, mutton, beef, or vegetables. *Harissa* is a condiment made of ground red pepper, garlic, and oil. *Brik* is a thin pancake stuffed with meat, eggs, or spinach, which is often sold by street vendors. Strong Turkish coffee and mint tea are popular. African lobster and all kinds of seafood and shellfish are plentiful along the coast.

**Housing:** Many years ago the Berbers built windowless houses called *ghorfas*, which were reached by mud stairs or ladders. Some exist today, but they are largely used for grain storage rather than for housing. In Matmata people live at the bottom of enormous holes more than 20 ft. (6 m) deep with mud walls that keep the dwellings warm in winter and cool in summer. The growing middle class of shopkeepers, bureaucrats, and teachers in the cities has caused a housing shortage. Most homes are small and are built of stone, adobe, or concrete because there is so little lumber available. In the country almost all houses are surrounded by a low wall. Nomads carry their "households" on their own backs or on those of their camels.

**Holidays:**

January 1, New Year's Day
January 18, National Revolution Day
March 20, Independence Day
April 9, Martyrs' Day
May 1, Labor Day
June 1, Victory Day
June 2, Youth Day
July 25, Republic Day
August 3, President's Birthday
August 13, Women's Day
September 3, Memorial Day
October 15, Evacuation Day

**Culture:** The arts are a mixture of Muslim and Western influences. There are strong French influences, but the government has encouraged the development of a national literature in Arabic. Traditional arts—especially pottery, woodworking, and textiles—are enjoying a revival. Mosaics—an ancient art—decorate the walls and floors of public buildings. Metalsmiths have been shaping copper into useful and decorative objects for many years.

There is also an effort to establish a national music. *Malouf* is a complex type of music that is played on lute and guitar. These are sad songs that are thought to derive from Arabian music brought to Spain in the eighth century and reexported to Tunisia in the seventeenth century when all Jews and Muslims were driven from Spain.

One of Tunisia's finest writers is a Jew, Albert Memmi, whose semiautobiographical novel, *The Pillar of Salt*, tells of Jewish family life.

Tunisia has a splendid museum, the Bardo, which has a large collection of Roman mosaics and Carthaginian antiquities.

**Communication:** Telecommunications are relatively well developed. Two of Tunis's four daily newspapers are printed in French.

**Transportation:** Tunisia had a relatively modern transportation system when it achieved independence in 1956, and it has improved considerably since then.

Railroads and well-constructed highways connect the larger cities. There are four major commercial seaports—at Tunis, Bizerte, Sousse, and Sfax—as well as a new major port complex at Gabes. The major cities are linked by air, and there are five international airports.

**Education:** Tunisian education has been modeled after the French system. There are six years of primary schooling followed by three of secondary. Some students then pursue either academic specialization or vocational training. Classes are conducted in French and Arabic, although Arabic is used increasingly. In 1858 a law made public education free at all levels, but school attendance is not mandatory. Girls make up half of the classes in the cities, but in rural areas many girls are confined to household tasks. Forty-five percent of Tunisian adults are unable to read. A university was founded in Tunisia in 1960 to replace an Institute of Higher Studies that had been established by the French. In 1986 universities were established also in Monastir and Sfax.

**Health and Welfare:** Health conditions are far from adequate, though they are improving. They compare favorably to those in other developing countries. Diseases of childhood and infancy constitute the major health problem. The average life expectancy is now approaching 60 years. Social security programs cover the majority of the work force. Old age, disability, and survivor pensions, compensation for sickness, maternity, and work injury, and free medical services are provided.

**Principal Products:**
*Agriculture:* Apricots, citrus fruits, grapes, tomatoes, corn, melons, olives, onions, potatoes, almonds, barley, wheat
*Mining:* Petroleum, phosphate rock
*Manufacturing:* Cork, textiles, leather goods, processed food and beverages

# IMPORTANT DATES

1200 B.C.—Phoenicians establish a colony near the site of present-day Tunis

814 B.C.—What we now know as Tunisia becomes the stronghold of the Phoenicians

264-241 B.C. — Carthage is defeated in the first Punic War

Third century B.C. — Tunis becomes the center of Roman power in North Africa

149 B.C. — Carthage is destroyed and is annexed to Rome; Julius Caesar orders that it be rebuilt

First and Second centuries A.D. — Many Jews are sent to Tunisia in exile after rebelling against Roman rule in Palestine

A.D. 429 — Geiseric, king of the Vandals, arrives in Africa

439 — Tunis is occupied by Vandals

455 — Vandals plunder Rome

533-34 — Tunis is won back by the Eastern Roman Empire

622 — Muhammad and his followers move from Mecca to Medina

632 — Muhammad dies

670 — Arabs sweep into Tunisia and begin conquering North Africa

712 — Arabs invade Spain

800s — Kairouan becomes a center of religious learning

1453 — Byzantine Empire in Constantinople collapses

1492 — Arab Muslims are driven out of Spain

1535 — Tunis is captured by Emperor Charles V

1573 — Tunis becomes a Turkish province

1704 — An Ottoman Turk of Cretan origin makes himself hereditary ruler

1757—Siali family receives 1,350 sq. mi. (3,497 km²) of land near Sfax

1830—France rules Algeria

1869—Financial control is established by England, France, and Italy

1878—England allows France free hand in Tunisia in return for French acquiescence in British occupation of Cyprus

1881—France establishes protectorate

1885—Land Registration Act passed; colonists flock to Tunisia

1907—Young Tunisian party is formed, which urges Tunisians to manage their own affairs

1934—Neo-Destour party is formed; Habib Bourguiba becomes secretary-general

1938—Bourguiba and his principal associates are again imprisoned

1942—Bourguiba is transferred to Vichy France; Bourguiba refuses to cooperate with Axis powers; Bourguiba is freed

1943—Germans are driven out of Tunisia; rule of Free French is restored

1952—Widespread violence breaks out against French control

1954—French premier Mendes-France agrees to grant internal autonomy

1956—Tunisia attains full independence; becomes member of United Nations

1957—Tunisia becomes a republic; Bourguiba is elected president

1963—The last French forces leave Tunisia

1982—Temporary headquarters of PLO is set up in Tunisia

1987—Tunisia breaks off diplomatic relations with Iran; Bourguiba is replaced as president by Prime Minister Zine el-Abidine Ben Ali

*A guard at the Bardo Palace*

# IMPORTANT PEOPLE

Ibrahim el-Aghlab (c. 902-?), ruled North Africa, established Hafsid Dynasty in Tunisia

St. Augustine (354-430), early Christian church father, philosopher, and writer

Belisarius (c. 505-565), Byzantine general, led expedition that overthrew Vandal kingdom in North Africa

Zine el-Abidine Ben Ali (1936-    ), prime minister; became president in 1987

Habib Bourguiba (1903-    ), president of Tunisia from 1957 to 1987

Geiseric, king of the Vandals

Hannibal (247-183 B.C.), Carthaginian general who crossed the Alps into Italy and defeated the Romans; in North Africa he was defeated by Scipio Africanus

Husain Ibn Ali, guaranteed the people protection and ruled with popular support

Justinian (483-565), Byzantine emperor and head of the Eastern Christian church

Kahina, Berber priestess

Mehmed (1432-1481), Ottoman sultan, called "The Conqueror," who established a Muslim Turkish kingdom

Albert Memmi (1920-    ), author

Pierre Mendes-France (1907-82), statesman, prime minister of France in 1954, proclaimed self government of Tunisia

Muhammad (c. 570-632), prophet who founded Islamic religion

Hedi Nourira, twentieth-century prime minister

Al Sadok Bey, nineteenth-century bey who signed treaty with France giving them temporary power that lasted seventy-five years

Sheikh Taalbi, leader of the Young Tunisians; wrote a book that set forth principles on which the Destour party was formed

Tertullian (150-?), scholar who created Latin Christian literature

Uqba ben Nafi, Arab commander who founded a military base south of Carthage around 670

*Berber women loading a donkey*

# INDEX

**Page numbers that appear in boldface type indicate illustrations**

## About the Author

Mary Virginia Fox was graduated from Northwestern University and now lives near Madison, Wisconsin, conveniently located across the lake from the state capital and the University of Wisconsin. She is the author of more than two dozen young adult books and a number of feature articles for adult publications.

Mrs. Fox and her husband lived for several months on the shores of the Mediterranean in the town of Carthage with a Roman pillar and a Phoenician "cannon ball" in their front yard. "To feel so close to history is a mesmerizing experience," says Mrs. Fox. "I closed my eyes and watched the past walk by."

j        Fox, Mary Virginia
916.1      Tunisia.
FOX